Suzie
OF COBTREE
FARM

Hannah Buckland

ACKNOWLEDGMENTS

I would like to thank my friend, Marilyn, for reading the manuscript and giving her wise and enthusiastic comments. Also, thank you to Rachel, my sister, for her interest and encouragement.

I would also like to thank Amos Adekayero and Jose Olapade of Christian Book Ltd for their professional and helpful service.

CHAPTER 1

The whole school rose to their feet to sing the hymn. Miss Maple's dainty fingers danced over the harmonium's keys as she improvised an elaborate introduction. As usual, she looked smugly satisfied with her own accomplishments. How unfortunate that her musical talents were as pearls before swine in this little backwater establishment!

Suzie stood, seething with rage and frustration. She could not bring herself to sing or even mouth the words:

Well-pleased the toiling swains behold,

The waving yellow crop.

With joy they bear the sheaves away,

And sow again in hope.

It wasn't the archaic language that irritated her so much, nor was it the poor poetry. It was the total inappropriateness of the words. How insensitive to expect the little village children to sing of a joyful harvest!

The music stopped suddenly, and Suzie's inner rantings were abruptly interrupted.

"Suzannah Griffen, you are not singing!" Miss Maple's high-pitched voice cut over the heads of the pupils, who turned as one to stare at the offender.

"No, I am not," replied Suzie, looking her teacher straight in the eye.

"And may I ask why not?" The shrill voice had gone up an octave.

Never before in her whole life had Suzie challenged a teacher's authority, but today was different. With sweaty palms but a steady voice, she answered.

"The harvest hymn you made us sing is totally inappropriate."

"How so?" asked Miss Maple icily. "It is harvest time. Is it not?"

"Yes, it is September," agreed Suzie, "but the harvest has been a disaster for us farmers. It has rained all summer. The hay and crops have rotted in the fields; our sheep and cattle are knee-deep in mud." She glanced around at the scared faces of her fellow village children, and this emboldened her to continue. "Without crops, we can't earn money, pay the rent, or...."

Suzie was choking up. She could not give Miss Maple or the posh towny children the satisfaction of seeing her cry.

"Thank you, Suzannah, for giving us a lecture on rural economics," replied the teacher in a soft but sarcastic tone, which produced a muffled giggle of approval from the townies. "I shall report your disobedience and insurrection to the school board of directors."

Her little sister, Elsie, looked like a scared rabbit as she stared at her with shocked, tear-filled eyes, but the sarcasm and sniggers had evaporated Suzie's fears.

"Do not trouble yourself, Miss Maple. I am leaving and won't be returning. You have nothing more you can teach me." Then, with as much dignity as she could muster, she collected her books, took her shawl from its peg, and exited the school building. She slammed the door behind her.

Suzie maintained her haste and composure the entire length of the high street and out of town, but as soon as she had passed the last house and turned off into the muddy lane that led to her village, she crumbled. The tears she had fought for so long flooded out, and she stumbled erratically along the uneven track. The walk home would take at least half an hour, probably longer due to the mud, but that was not long enough to consider the consequences of her rash actions. So, Suzie made a detour and squelched her way across a meadow until she came to a disused cowshed. Throwing herself down on a pile of musty hay, Suzie laid back, shut her eyes in despair, and considered her situation.

Until the previous year, all the village girls had acquired a suitably minimal education in the dame school of a wise widow. In her own cottage, Mrs Jones had taught generations of village girls to read enough to follow a recipe, calculate enough to manage housekeeping money, and write enough to structure a simple love letter. As well as those modest accomplishments, her pupils learnt to identify every herb in her garden and know their therapeutic properties. Her girls could sew neat seams, knit warm socks, and turn worn collars. In short, the young women learnt all that they needed for the lives they were destined for—domestic service and matrimony.

But last winter, Mrs Jones contracted pneumonia, which refused to be remedied by her own apothecary skills or those of her formal pupils. Within a few weeks of getting ill, the shrewd woman, who was treated as an angel by half the villagers and a witch by the other half but was respected by all, died. Girls now had to join their brothers in walking three miles to the town school. The market town of Milford geographically lay a mere three miles from their rural village of Brookfield, but it felt like a different world. Milfordites were not dependent on the land for their wages but could boast of a paper mill, a respectable coaching inn, and a sizable row of shops. Milfordites despised Brookfield dwellers as grubby, uncouth country bumpkins—and none more so than the Milford pupils.

Before setting out on their walk to school, most of the Brookfield children had already helped with the farming and household chores. Dainty Milford pupils did not hold back; they laughed and wrinkled their noses at the villagers' muddy boots and patched-up frocks. Sniggering at the rural odours the steaming coats gave off as they dried by the stove, they even giggled when the villagers struggled with their grammar or geometry exercises. But, Miss Maple did not reprimand them.

Suzie hated Milford school, Milford children, and Miss Maple. She was the only older girl from Brookfield, for all her schoolfriends had gradually been withdrawn from education by their impoverished parents and sent into service. As the oldest villager, she felt isolated and picked on. Miss Maple basked in the adoration of her pupils and instinctively knew that Suzie would not succumb to her charms. Suzie saw straight through her petty little ways to her proud, vindictive heart. As well as looking after herself, Suzie tried to shield the younger villagers from the rough end of Miss Maple's sarcastic, sugary tongue and the town children's fists.

She slowly extracted herself from the hay. How was she going to explain the events to her parents? She knew they had sacrificed a lot to let her stay at school for so long. All her village friends were now either in service and sending home their wages or working on their family farms and homes. Last autumn, after harvest, her older brother John had been indentured as an apprentice to a wheelwright. Lads his age could earn as much as their fathers as manual labourers. Still, Suzie's parents had chosen not only to forgo that useful source of income, but also to pay out for his indenture and give him an opportunity they never had. Papa worked all hours on his rented farm, Cobtree Farm, and had just experienced the worst summer in living memory, and now she was about to disappoint him!

After careful consideration, Suzie lingered in the lanes until lunch time, when both her parents would be at home. To go through the same story twice would be very tiring. As she neared the house, another possibility struck her—what if her parents insisted that she return to school tomorrow!? She slowed her pace still further. She could never go back to face Miss Maple or the awful Milfordites! She imagined her father's grieved face and her mother's annoyance and almost ground to a halt. At the garden gate, she squared her shoulders and headed resolutely towards the kitchen door.

CHAPTER 2

Mrs Lydia Griffen clung to the kitchen worktop to steady herself. She desperately needed something to eat. All morning, since sunrise, she has been on her feet and busy. Mondays were her least favourite day of the week. Someone in the distant past must have deemed it a suitable day to do the laundry, but it seemed like a thoughtless decision. Or maybe just a male one. What women needed on a Monday was a catch-up day. The combination of doing the bare minimum of chores on the Sabbath, plus having one's children and husband around all day, meant that Monday mornings always saw the house looking rather higgle-de-piggle-de. Sunday dinner was always either a casserole prepared on Saturday evening or a cold meat meal. Monday dinners were supposed to be leftovers, but that assumed you could afford a nice big joint to roast for Sunday dinner, with plenty left for the following day. She could not possibly stretch for such luxuries, and even if she could, surely it would be breaking the Sabbath to spend it toiling away in the kitchen. Women would have to miss the morning service to keep the range stoked enough to roast potatoes! No, whoever invented washday Mondays was a rich, Sabbath-breaking man!

'On Mondays, I must have breakfast,' Lydia told herself severely. This morning, the children seemed famished, and it was easy to busy herself so that no one suspected she had gone without food. Her husband, Matthew, up and out early to earn extra money apple picking for the estate, had assumed she would eat with the children. The children probably didn't think anything, but if they did, they would assume she had eaten with their father. Matthew was the breadwinner; he needed feeding first. The children were growing and needed to keep their strength up. She would survive. Dipping a ladle into the churn, Lydia helped herself to a few mouthfuls of creamy, fresh milk. That would keep her going until midday, like it so often did.

At least, it was a good drying day. Lydia pegged out the washing and felt the contentment unique to having a line of fresh linen flapping on a line. She looked up at the birds overhead. "No deposits today, please!" she pleaded. After she had picked up the linen basket, she allowed herself to stand still and enjoy the September sun on her face. As she absorbed the sun's warmth, her contentment blossomed into thankfulness. Life may be tough and relentless, but her husband and children were healthy—and lovely. She looked at their three cows sitting contentedly, chewing the cud under an apple tree, and then at the sheep grazing peacefully. They were all happy and not fearing the future, and she must be the same. God had never promised anyone an easy life, but He had promised His presence and help—and for these, she prayed.

The click of the garden gate jolted Lydia into action—Matthew was home and required prompt feeding before he returned to the orchard. Gathering up her skirts, she ran down the path to the kitchen door. Her eyes took a while to adjust to the darkness as she descended to the cool cellar for butter and cheese. The bread was old and dry, but a bit of butter or a quick dunk in the teacup, would make it palatable. Matthew was always grateful for whatever she set before him, but she did wish she could give him fresh bread every day.

Matthew had only just finished saying grace when Suzie burst in. Lydia was used to her dramatic entrances, but not at midday. Her parents listened to Suzie's tale in grim silence. Their bread and cheese lunch was left untouched during her tearful explanation. Having blurted out the details, Suzie fell silent. *Probably waiting for an eruption of parental wrath, thought Lydia.* Instead, she and Matthew exchanged a knowing look. Their quick-eyed daughter detected it,

"Has someone told you all this already?" she asked, irritated.

"No," replied her mother, "but we guessed there would soon be a bust-up between you and Miss Maple sooner or later. You and your impulsive nature."

"More like her snooty ways," argued Suzie, "and I am not going back!"

Matthew pushed back his chair and put his hands on the armrests. *Now, I am in for a lecture*, thought Suzie.

"No, you will not go back, Suzie," he said soberly. "Earlier this month, your mother and I reluctantly decided that, due to the bad harvest, we should pull you out of school and find you a domestic position to help the family purse."

Suzie could not believe her luck! Not going back to school, getting a job, and earning money!?

"How wonderful!" She enthused as she jumped up to kiss her Pa.

But her joy was dampened by his sorrowful face.

"We didn't want you to leave home yet, Suzie-girl. You are still young, impressionable, and impulsive."

"We will miss you and your help with the animals and children, too," agreed Ma.

"Where will I work?"

"Beggars can't be choosers, but I will enquire for you at the big house. The main thing is, we want the Lord to open up a way for you and protect you."

As Suzie put the next basket of wet washing through the mangle, she thought about the big house. Though less than a mile away, it was surrounded by a large, private park and glamorous mystery. The ornate mansion was the seat of local power. The inhabitants owned all they surveyed and much more beside. Their estate included Milford, Brookfield, all the farms between, and various hamlets beyond. Lord D'Egerton had a seat in Parliament (which was rarely sat on) and owned a Scottish estate, where, rumour had it, he had a castle. The D'Egerton's London house was in the expensive and fashionable Belgravia. Dotted along the lanes on either side of Brookfield village were the estate's tenanted farms.

Each farmhouse was identical. The front gable had white weatherboards with a middle front door, a small, open porch bearing the D'Egerton family crest, and a window on each side, top and bottom. Suzie thought they looked like happy houses with a pig's snout for a door. As one entered, there was a very small hallway, stairs going up directly ahead, a door to the sitting room to the left, and a door to the dining room on the right. Behind the front rooms, spanning the whole width was a spacious kitchen. The kitchens had four doors—one to the yard outside, one to a cellar, one to the dining room, and one to the sitting room. On a wet day, Lydia let the children see how many circles they could run, going through each room. Upstairs, there were three bedrooms. The courtyard outside had a water pump and trough, a washroom, and a log shed. Beyond that, the tenants could build their own farm building at their own expense, subject to written permission. Matthew's father had built stables, a small workshop, and a large barn.

Although the D'Egertons (or The Family, as they were locally known) were frequently away from their country residence, their firm but benevolent rule was constantly felt. If a cottage front garden became unbecomingly overgrown, the weatherboarding discoloured, or anything else became unsightly, a message was dispatched from The Great House, and the offender dealt with it forthwith. What would happen if the message was ignored was never discovered, for no one would dream of disobeying M'Lord.

The D'Egerton carriage was rarely seen in humble Brookfield. Maybe the muddy lanes and farmyard smells were deemed unsuitable for the nobility's sensibilities, but Brookfield's church was even more repulsive to them. The town and village were not only divided by wealth but also by religious leanings. Milford was high church and Brookfield low. For years, Suzie thought this referred to the height of their respective towers, but over the years, her father explained it was more than that. The Brookfield services were plain and simple, or as Pa put it, 'reformed and biblical', whereas the Milford services were as ornate as the Gothic church itself. With disgust, Pa explained that they used incense, candles, and rituals. They called their minister a priest and had an altar. "Roman Catholic in all but name!" grumbled Pa. "Before you know it, they will be offering confessionals and selling indulgencies."

The following evening, Suzie's father wandered down the lane to talk to John Green, a neighbour who was an undergardener for the D'Egertons. He promised to put in a word for Suzie the next time he delivered vegetables to the kitchen door. The days passed, and Suzie despaired of ever receiving any answer, let alone a positive one. But finally, a fortnight later, Mr Green plodded into the farmyard and found Mr Griffen. Suzie saw him approach as she was gathering in the washing. Leaving the task unfinished, she hid behind the haystack where she could listen unobserved.

For a long time, it seemed that Mr Green had only come to discuss the weather and milk prices, but eventually, after clearing his throat, he began,

"Now, about ya young Suzie, I asked at te big 'ouse, and te only job going is fa a scullery maid. They don't last five minutes, them maids."

Her father thanked his friend for the information, but his face did not look thankful, only sad. As soon as Mr Green had departed, Suzie skipped over to her father.

"There's a job for me then?" she sang.

Mr Griffen leant on his pitchfork. "Yes, there is one, Suzie. But it isn't what I wanted for you, my girl. A scullery maid's job is real skivvy work."

"I can skivvy, Pa. Ma always says I am a work horse."

Her father opened his mouth to answer, but Suzie never heard his reply, for her mother was calling from the kitchen window.

"Suzie! The goat is heading for the washing basket!!"

Matthew shook his head. How he would miss his eldest daughter!

CHAPTER 3

Lydia's wish to keep her daughter for a few more weeks was so intense that it was a physical ache. Suzie was handy to have around the house and farmyard. She was never happier than when she was working with the animals in her scruffy clothes and hair in long, messy plaits. It was hard to imagine that next week, Suzie would be stuck in a hot kitchen, corseted in a prim uniform, with her hair in a tight bun. Due to the wet weather, the harvest was poor, but there were still the apples and potatoes to harvest, hedgerow fruits to jam, and vegetables to pickle. Despite it only being September, the prospect of winter already loomed in her mind's eye, and she wanted to be ready. Matthew would normally help with the apples and potatoes, but he was working all hours on the estate, making the most of the casual work on offer.

During the hop-picking season, he had become a tally man, spending long days going around the dusty hop gardens, measuring and recording how many bushels of hops each family had picked into their hessian bins. The pickers were paid by the bushel, so his reckonings determined their wages. The tallied hops were tipped into pokes and taken to the oast house for drying. His was an unenviable role, for he could please no one—the hoppers moaned that he measured too harshly and tried every trick known to man to make their picking volume seem greater. The dryer in the oast house complained if he was working too slowly—the coal fires used to dry the hops needed constant tending, and a late filling of a kiln would mean working into the small hours, and the foreman tutted if his tallying seemed too generous. Despite looking exhausted, Matthew insisted on picking apples every night after the evening meal. Lydia worried about him.

But potatoes had to be harvested earlier in the day. She and Suzie dug them in the mornings, leaving them on the damp soil to dry in the sun and turning them at noon to dry on the other side. Many of the potatoes had turned to mush in the rain-sodden ground, and they couldn't afford to waste more by bagging them up damp.

Every day after school, Elsie and Charlie changed into their dirty farm clothes and helped lay the potatoes and apples on straw in the attic. Throughout the winter, it would be Charlie's job to catch up with the semi-feral farm cats a few times a week and shut them in the attic to do some mousing. No one could understand why they struggled and scratched despite rich earnings when they were up there!

As she dug the potatoes, Lydia thought about her brood. John, far away, is learning a trade. Although he was miles away from her, it was John she worried about the least. He seemed like a steady, sensible lad. His boss was a good, religious man whose wife was kind and cheerful. John would be safe under their roof. After John, Suzie had come as a bit of a shock. Lydia imagined she had mastered motherhood until Suzie arrived. John had been a quiet, thoughtful toddler who you could plonk into a wash basket with a few toys or picture book while you got on with housework and know he would stay put. Suzie was completely different. She wouldn't stay in one place long enough for you to collect the toys and books. If she was put in the basket, she would clamber out. If you left her out of the basket, she would climb in. Sitting quietly through a church service, sucking her thumb, or falling asleep was not Suzie's style. Lydia used to feel smug as John snuggled onto her knee and sat quietly until he fell asleep, while other babies fretted about and had to be taken out. Then she had Suzie!

But for all Suzie's naughtiness, Lydia adored her. Her lively, inquisitive nature made her a delight to observe. She watched Suzie growing up with interest, sometimes not knowing whether to laugh or cry at her escapades. After Suzie, three more babies may have joined the family, but their lives were not to be. In each case, within the first few months of knowing she was pregnant, Lydia felt the ominous grip of severe abdominal pain, which eventually ripped her tiny baby from her, leaving her drained and devastated. Despairing of ever mothering another child, Lydia threw all her efforts into bringing up John and Suzie and, as her strength returned, helping on the farm.

The dreaded signs of pregnancy crept upon her once again, and fearing to acknowledge them even to herself, she hid the fact from Matthew as long as possible. She waited and waited for the sickening pain to overtake her, but the weeks passed, and nothing happened. When her state could no longer be hidden, everyone was delighted except herself. Unable to believe she would receive a live, healthy baby at full term, she could not allow herself to rejoice until little Elsie was safely delivered and in her arms. She had gazed at her tiny daughter's beautiful limbs and perfect fingers and toes, wondering at the miracle of new life. Right from the start, Elsie seemed to realise that her mother was a busy woman and tried to cause as little work as possible. Dear Elsie, always so sweet, shy, and cautious! Sending her off to school had been such a wrench, even with John and Suzie to protect and carry her. Lydia still remembered those first mornings of waving them off: Elsie's turned face and pleading eyes locking her gaze, getting further and further away, as Suzie piggy-backed her down the lane. Lydia struggled to maintain her faltering smile until they were out of sight before burying her teary face into baby Charlie's tummy and making him chuckle. Charlie had been called 'Baby Charlie' for far too long. Being the youngest, he had probably been a bit spoilt by all. His angelic face belied his cheeky character. His older siblings had pandered to him as soon as he could make his wishes known, which was at a surprisingly young age. Giving him what he wanted was easier than dealing with the loud and long protests he could produce, and he rewarded them with the sunniest smile imaginable. Lydia was secretly relieved when she finally waved her youngest off to school. He was more than ready for the challenge, had all his older siblings there to keep an eye on him, and now Lydia could get on with her daily chores unimpeded by his continuous volley of questions and theorising. She wished the teacher well!

All too soon, the dreaded day arrived. Suzie looked so capable and mature, with her hair in a neat bun and dressed in her Sunday best, that Lydia felt proud despite all her sadness. Her daughter deserved this opportunity for betterment, to see more of the world, and to know the pleasure of earning a wage, even if she would keep very little for herself. Suzie's wages would barely touch her pocket before they were handed over to her parents. The extra income would be welcome to feed the family and go towards John's apprenticeship fees. A slight twinge of unfairness gripped Lydia's heart, but she could not waste her energy on such a universal truth—boys come first. After a hasty, early breakfast, which both Suzie and Lydia struggled to eat, Matthew prayed earnestly for Suzie's well-being, then instructed his daughter to fetch her bonnet and shawl. There was no point in lingering over their farewells, so after a brief hug and kiss, Lydia let her oldest daughter go. As she watched Matthew and Suzie hurry down the lane and disappear around the corner, Lydia wondered, *Would Suzie ever live at home again, or was this the end of this chapter of family life?* Inside the cottage, Elsie was squeaking—Charlie was probably pulling her pigtails or up to another of his annoying tricks. Lydia sighed. During the brief moments, she had walked up the garden path to deal with the antagonist. Lydia silently prayed again for Suzie. Seeing her this morning, all smart in her pretty frock, her corset tightened to create a more ladylike silhouette, and her hair under control, a new worry was born in Lydia's mind: her little daughter was now a young woman, and she may attract attention from the opposite sex.

A walk with Pa was normally an enjoyable experience. He pointed out various trees and plants and had interesting stories about the cottages and farms they passed, but today was different. His comments seemed forced, and she struggled to concentrate. As their feet relentlessly propelled them along the lanes, she felt sick with dread. Every minute, they were getting nearer the moment they had to part, and she would be left with a bunch of strangers. She had always loved her dear old Pa, but just now, that love had swelled so much that it nearly burst her heart. He was such a steady, reliable presence in her life, and soon, he would not be present. She may not see him again for months. Homelife would carry on in its normal manner, and she would not be there. Her place at the table would be empty. Elsie would have the bed to herself and have no one to warm her toes. Everything inside her cried out to stop moving and plead with Pa to turn around, but he was talking.

"Remember all we have taught you, Suzie-girl. Read your Bible and pray every day. Shun bad language and bad company."

"Yes, Pa."

"I don't know what the staff are like, but they're probably a mixed bunch. Watch 'em and bide your time before you offer them your confidence and friendship."

"Yes, Pa." Suzie couldn't trust her voice to say more, and they walked along in silence. The birds sang as if it were a normal day.

"And do as you are told by your superiors. They don't want your ideas, just your obedience."

Suzie could not imagine what life would be like. She wondered if her father did. His gaze at her was so serious, grave, and loving that tears welled up and threatened to overflow. Only children were allowed to cry. She was no longer a child but a bread-winning woman. She had to do this for the family. She blinked and sniffed hard.

"Your mother would say, 'Don't sniff. Use your hankie,'" smiled Pa, lightening the moment. Taking her little hand into his big, hardened one, he gave it a reassuring squeeze. They walked hand in hand until, turning a corner in the road, they sighted the grand mansion. Its size and opulence made Suzie gasp.

"And this is just the side view. We're heading up the tradesman's drive. The family and guests would get an even more impressive sight."

"I can't imagine anything more impressive."

"Imagine riding in a fine carriage down an oak-lined drive, entering an ornate garden with bushes cut into clever shapes. Alighting at a massive front door with marble steps leading up to it and marble pillars at the porch."

"It's a different world."

"That is for sure."

"But I would prefer home," mused Suzie wistfully.

Their boots crunched along the stone driveway, and the house loomed closer and closer.

"Whenever I see this edifice and imagine the life of luxury inside it, I always think of the text: 'What will it profit a man if he gains the whole world and loses his own soul?' This won't last forever, Suzie, but the mansion in the skies will."

"Yes," answered Suzie automatically. She was far too distracted to attend to her father's sermonising. This was to be where she lived and worked. Was she up to it?

Her parting from Pa was far too quick and perfunctory. He had a long walk home, then a day's work ahead of him, and the housekeeper seemed impatient to get Suzie uniformed up and introduced to the cook. As she scurried after the formidable woman through a maze of dark passages, she imagined her father getting further and further away. How she longed to drop her trunk and run after him! How would she ever get to know her way around the corridors and long, winding stairs?

"What's your name, girl?" The housekeeper asked as she ascended the stairs at a fearsome rate.

"Suzanna Griffen, Ma'am," panted Suzie.

"Well, we'll call you 'Anna' for short."

"My family always calls me Suzie."

The housekeeper stopped and swung around.

"We are NOT your family, and you will be known as Anna. Suzie sounds frivolous. Do I make myself clear?"

"Yes, Mrs…. Er, Ma'am."

"Mrs Benson is the name."

"Yes, Mrs Benson."

The housekeeper stopped at the door, which looked identical to many others.

"This is your room. You are sharing with Mabel, the lower kitchen maid. Put your trunk on your bed. Get your uniform on. See me in my housekeeping room as soon as possible." Her sentences were short and clipped as if multiplying words on a scullery maid would be wasting her precious time. As she swung out the door, Suzie timidly called after her.

"Mrs Benson, how can I find your room?"

"Down four flights of stairs, turn right, second left, third door on the left. And be sharp."

Four stairs, right, 2nd left, 3rd door on the left. Four stairs, right, 2nd left, 3rd door on the left. Suzie could think of nothing else as she slipped out of her frock and pulled on her uniform, apron, and cap. Peering into the looking glass, she met the gaze of a pale, scared girl dressed in an oversized outfit, which, though washed, still smelt of its previous owner. Suzie scrapped all her loose hair ends under the unbecoming cap, gave herself an encouraging smile, and set off to find her boss.

Suzie's only mistake was to enter the linen store cupboard instead of the housekeeper's room, but no one noticed, and she was secretly pleased with her own success and quickness.

"About time, too!" muttered Mrs Benson as Suzie entered her lair.

Barely having time to notice the cosiness of the room, Suzie was ushered out and along more corridors to meet the woman who would control her every waken moment—the cook herself. Suzie had heard awful rumours about cooks—they could be malicious ogres who made their underlings' lives a misery. Cooks were known for their exacting standards and short fuses. Or would it be a male French chef—very fashionable, formidable, and fiery?

Great was Suzie's relief when she met the cook—Mrs MacPherson. The round little woman, engulfed in a massive, bespattered apron and a ready smile, welcomed her warmly. Her lilting Scottish accent was soothing and homely. Suzie immediately knew she could trust and like her boss.

"E, ya a wee lass, but I hope ya handy."

"I'll work hard, Mrs MacPherson." Suzie wanted so much to please her.

"Call me 'Mrs Mackie'. Everybody does."

"Best you do is work hard," barked Mrs Benson. "Our last few scullery maids have hardly lasted a couple of months. Shockingly inept!"

"'Our scullery maids?' Mrs Benson," cut in Mrs Mackie icily. "I would be grateful if you remembered that the kitchen and the kitchen staff are my concern."

"I'll remind you of that, Mrs MacPherson, when this girl proves to be a disappointment and needs dismissal! You didn't even interview her, just because you know her father. How business-like is that?"

Suzie felt terribly awkward.

"I'll…"

"Silence," barked Mrs Benson, "never speak to your superiors until asked. Never interrupt a conversation!"

Mrs Benson flounced across the kitchen. "Good luck with your next protégé, Mackie!" Bang!

The housekeeper exited, taking the icy atmosphere with her.

"Annoying woman!" smiled Mrs Mackie. "Anna, put on the kettle— the small one—and we'll have a quick coffee before preparing lunch."

At the ring of a handbell, two other maids appeared from another kitchen. Kitty, the first kitchen maid, was Mrs Mackie's right-hand man. Over two years, she had progressed from peeling vegetables and gutting fowl to preparing the servant's food. Now, she had been promoted to helping feed The Family. She was well on her way to perfecting sauces and souffles. Soon, she would be proficient enough to spread her wings and apply for a cook's position herself. Ruby, the second maid, was responsible for feeding the servants with basic, cheap, but nutritious meals. This was no mean feat, as there were normally about thirty hungry mouths to feed. Mabel, the lower housemaid and Suzie's bedfellow, assisted Ruby and was at everyone else's beck and call.

As soon as her coffee cup was empty, Suzie learnt her role. Just off the main kitchen on the left were a wet kitchen, a still room, and a cool room. To the right was a scullery with two large sinks, wooden draining boards, and a large wheezing geezer to heat the water. This was Suzie's domain. The chill of the stone floor soon penetrated through her boot soles as she leaned over the deep sinks to scrub the pans. Above the sinks were large, barred windows, but they were so high that all that could be seen was the sky. Suzie wondered what the bars were for. If she wanted to escape, she would surely use the door, and why on earth would anyone want to enter the scullery voluntarily? The whitewashed walls were grimy from the smoke of the fire that heated the geezer, splattered with fat from the cooking pans, and damp with the steam of the hot water.

Suzie's task was to scrub the cooking and baking equipment. All the greasiest, muckiest pots and pans, cauldrons and cullenders, ladles and lids, beaters and beakers. As soon as Mrs Mackie had finished with a bowl or utensil, Suzie was to whisk it away and ensure it was sparkling clean, ready for the next time it was required. All the servants' tableware came to the scullery, but The Family's delicate crockery, fine silver cutlery, and cut crystal glassware were washed by the footmen in the butler's pantry. The only articles of smart crockery decorated with the family crest that Suzie ever saw were the huge platters, jugs, and serving dishes that were sent down to be warmed and filled. And even then, she only saw them. Kitty strictly forbade anyone except herself and Mrs Mackie from touching them—"A year's wages won't pay for a replacement for even an eggcup!" *We treat them like the crown jewels,* thought Suzie, as she admired them from a respectful distance.

CHAPTER 4

Lydia tried not to feel lonesome as she singlehandedly fed the chickens and milked the cows. The mornings were getting colder and darker. Lydia always felt under pressure during September and October. The harvest in the garden, orchard, and hedgerow would not wait, and whatever wasn't gathered would go to waste. Winter loomed ahead, and her brood needed feeding throughout the cold, barren months. This year, Lydia felt the pressure even more keenly. Their small savings had dwindled rapidly over the past twelve months, and more expenses were likely. They would need to purchase seed for next year and may even need to buy animal fodder for the winter. Lydia prayed for an Indian summer to dry the saturated ground and speed up the grass growth for a little longer. Hay-making in October was almost unheard of, but if she could cut and dry a bit more, it would certainly help. Animals always preferred hay made early in the summer, but beggars could not be choosers. The burden that hung over the family daily was the rent. Keeping up the rent payments was the one thing that kept them housed and in a viable business. Was their farm viable? This was the question that only time could answer.

Matthew continued finding work on the estate farm. After the hop-picking had ended, he went straight on to apple picking. As the days grew shorter, he had less and less time after the evening meal to work on his own acres. Lydia had skills she could use to generate a little income. Having been a seamstress's assistant for many years, she could sew fast and neatly. She could alter clothes, turn collars, and make good buttonholes. She could advertise her skills when she took produce to Milford Market. But was she still skilled enough for the picky Milford clientele? How would she price her work? And above all, where would she find the time to sew? She hardly sat down from dawn to dusk, and when she finally slumped in an armchair just before bedtime, she was far too exhausted to do intricate stitching. Her eyesight at that time of the night wasn't at its best either.

Lydia remembered all her years in the small workroom behind Mrs Price's shop. She had traipsed along the muddy lane for twelve long years, from her parents' cottage in Brookfield to Milford, to sit all day bend over her sewing. Her neck and shoulders ached just thinking about it! If she was lucky, Mrs Price would take an afternoon off to 'go calling', and Lydia would be trusted to sell a few ribbons or buttons in her absence. Anything more demanding was not to be attempted, and Lydia had to write down the customer's name and request and promise it would be dealt with 'forthwith'. As a young girl of fourteen, Lydia already hated the job, but she kept quiet, knowing it was her parents' wish to learn a trade and that she was not allowed to express her personal opinion on such matters. Her dreamy hope was that Mr Right would soon appear and relieve her from her drudgery. But Mr Right made no such appearance. She lost count of the number of bride's dresses she had helped to sew for her friends. By this time, she was an accomplished seamstress herself, and some villagers suggested that she wanted to be a professional woman rather than a wife. How hurtful that was! She was only skilled because she had been so long in the job and through no choice of her own.

Then, one December evening, things started to change. Lydia had been reluctant to attend the village carol singing. Not because she disliked carols—indeed, quite the opposite was true—but because she knew that none of her old friends would be there. They would all be caring for their little ones at their own firesides. She was rather shy of the boisterous and confident youths below her age and suspected them of scorning her for her singleness. She would have gladly sat at home with a book, but her mother had encouraged her to make the effort.

"They are relying on your alto voice, my dear."

"No one will miss me."

"The tunes need good singers."

"I am not talking about my voice, but me as a person. No one cares tuppence if I am there or not."

"Mrs Huggins will be pleased to see you."

"Just so she can complain about her rheumatism to someone who isn't rushing off to speak with another person."

"She wonders if you are becoming somewhat of a recluse."

"A recluse!" Lydia sprang from her chair as if she had sat on a sewing needle. "How rude that woman is. I AM going tonight!" And with that, she flounced out of the room. As she changed into her best winter dress and selected a bonnet and warm shawl that matched, she rued the lot of single women—spurned by men, misunderstood by women, and sneered at by youths. Everyone was clear and doctrinal on the subject of providence, except where it applies to marriage!

Running late and still feeling hurt, Lydia inconspicuously joined herself to the crowd of carol singers. All the carol sheets had been handed out, but not wanting to draw attention to herself, Lydia reckoned she knew the words well enough to manage without them. Anyway, her lamp light had flickered and gone out, so she had nothing to illuminate the page. The lack of light suited her well, half hidden in the darkness. Hence, she could look around at the gathered throng without being noticed. Or so she thought. Suddenly, there was a gentle tap on her arm. Swinging around, Lydia found herself looking into the eyes of Matthew Griffen. Lydia had never made eye contact with him before, let alone held any form of conversation.

"Would you care to share my carol sheets, Miss Hobden?"

"I know most of the words; thank you," replied Lydia.

"There are some new ones this year."

Lydia stopped herself; she had sounded guarded and icy. Looking into her companion's brown eyes, she knew he didn't deserve her shortness.

"Thank you. It would be a great help, Mr Griffen, and stupidly, I didn't fill up my lamp either."

"Well, you hold the words, and I'll hold my lamp."

"Thank you." She flashed him a brief smile and was rewarded with a warm one in return.

As the singers sang their way through 'Silent Night', Lydia mindlessly joined in. Under her navy bonnet, her mind was working overtime. She knew the Griffens—they were a quiet family from Cobtree Farm, on the outskirts of the village. Her family and theirs had little to do with each other—the Griffens being several years older than her and her siblings. They attended the chapel but sat in the gallery and had always slipped out straight after the benediction—probably to tend their stock. The Griffens were never very sociable and always seemed busy working. All the Griffen offspring had left home except Matthew, who now ran the farm. No one knew much about Matthew. He wasn't interesting enough for people to talk about. He was just a bachelor who worked hard and lived with his elderly parents. Lydia thought hard, *"Had his mother died or not?"* She couldn't remember and felt awkward about that.

Glancing sideways, Lydia peeped shyly at Matthew. All wrapped up in a fur hat and woollen scarf, there wasn't much of his face she could see. But the limited amount she saw seemed totally engrossed in the job at hand. There is no whirling mind under his hat, she thought. And he was doing a good job of the singing, too. His voice had a deep, melodious base, which seemed to circle and blend effortlessly around her alto notes. The sound of their combined singing pleased Lydia. Carols always gladdened her heart— the wonderful news of a Saviour, the amazement of His incarnation, hopes of heaven, mixed with a seasonal feeling of nostalgia. But now, suddenly, she knew she was not only enjoying the past and looking forward to the eternal future, but also the present. She felt a deep happiness inside, which she hadn't experienced for a long time. At the end of the carol, Lydia found herself grinning, and Matthew was smiling back.

"I believe you enjoy singing, Miss Hobden."

"I really do, do you?"

Moving with the crowd, they headed for the next cluster of houses.

"I do. You have a beautiful voice."

"So do you." Lydia, annoyed to find herself blushing, lowered her head and let her bonnet hide her face.

"Thanks, but can a male voice be called beautiful?" smiled Matthew.

Everyone had stopped.

"Christians Awake!" shouted Mr Timmins.

"Is that a command or suggestion?" whispered Matthew.

Lydia giggled.

"Christians Awake. Number 23. To the normal tune."

As Lydia found the number, she found the word.

"Sonorous."

"Excuse me?" queried Matthew.

"That would describe a beautiful male voice, wouldn't it? Sonorous."

"To describe Mr Timmins?"

Lydia glanced at Matthew again. *There is more to this man than I thought*, she decided. *I do believe he has a sense of humour.*

"Yes, Mr Timmins, indeed." She quickly teased back just as the said man blasted out the first nasal note, and everybody joined in.

Carol singing was always a long, drawn-out affair. Mr Timmins, the organiser, was so determined to treat all villagers fairly and to sing to every cottage, however remote, that everyone was chilled to the bone, sore in the throat, and weary of walking by the time they reached the last hamlet. But this year, the chill and miles seemed like nothing to Lydia. In fact, she wished they could sing to all of Milford too. She and Matthew were not engaged in a steady stream of conversation. In fact, they spent most of their walking time in silence, but it was a companionable silence. What few comments he did make were always apt, interesting, and witty. Lydia felt comfortable and happy.

"That was our final carol," announced the strident (rather than sonorous) voice of Mr Timmins. "You are all most welcome back to our home for the customary cup of tea and slice of my wife's best Christmas cake."

This was the moment Lydia had been dreading! Standing around was much more awkward than walking. Also, Mrs Timmins and Mrs Huggins would lurk inside with their teapots, observing eyes and gossiping tongues. Matthew and Lydia slowly made their way to the Timmins' cottage, along with the rest of the singers. At the garden gate, Matthew stopped.

"And this is where I must leave you, I'm afraid. I need to get back to Pa. Since mother's death, he has found the long evenings rather difficult, and I don't want to leave him alone for too long."

Lydia felt relieved.

"Actually," she replied, "I don't usually go to this bit. I would normally sneak home myself."

"Really? Surely you are not as unsociable as a Griffen, are you?" asked Matthew, sounding quite pleased.

"Heading that way," smiled Lydia.

"Then let me walk you home."

"You aren't going that way."

Matthew started walking in the direction of her house. "Who says I am not? Anyway, you don't have a working lamp."

Suzie opened her mouth but closed it again. She realised an argument would clearly be futile, and anyway, she didn't particularly want to argue.

That evening's walk together was the first of many. The walks developed into courtship, the courtship into an engagement, and an engagement into a marriage. The local gossips saw it as a marriage of convenience. Matthew and his father needed a housekeeper and would be hard-pressed to pay wages, and Lydia, the spinster, needed an escape from her sewing room. But the Huggins and Timmins of this world could sourly speculate all they liked. Lydia loved Matthew with all her heart and was left in no doubt at all that her love was fully reciprocated.

Lydia smiled as she dragged her mind back to the present day. She had now been happily married for seventeen years. Much had changed during that time—their brood had been born, her father-in-law had died, but much had stayed the same—Matthew's phlegmatic humour, the farm itself, and most of the furniture in the house.

CHAPTER 5

Caleb Baker shut the door of his parent's farmhouse behind him and sucked in a lung full of pure Scottish highland air. He smiled to himself as he strolled down the path towards the steading. Nowhere in the whole world was more beautiful and majestic on a cold autumn morning than Taitneach, his valley, or Strath, as the locals would call it. The rapidly moving clouds changed the colour of the majestic mountain peaks from purple to brown to grey, then back again. The hills, decked with yellow gorse, purple heather, and golden bracken, became first threatening, then inviting, over and over again as the shadows rolled across them. Today, the visibility was good. Far up the valley, Caleb could see the waterfall silently and gently cascading down the mountainside. The water sparkled as it tumbled over the rocks. By late winter and during the spring, its mood would change, and the waters would thunder down in an angry torrent. Its roar could be heard from anywhere in the valley. The gentle brook that flowed through the glen became foaming, fierce, and dangerous.

But Caleb had no time to muse on the moods of the valley. Autumn would swiftly turn into winter, and there was plenty to do before the weather cut the valley off from the rest of the world. The sheep, who had been wandering the mountain ranges during the mild summer months, needed rounding up and bringing down to the sheltered valley fields to winter and lamb.

Rounding up the sheep required plenty of manpower, so all of Caleb's brothers and a few older nephews would be involved. No one was expected to attend school during the round-up. The Bakers would have been called a clan had they been Scottish. But unlike the Campbells and MacLeods, the Bakers were Englishmen. Another two hundred years or so of dwelling in Scotland were required before they would be considered anything but newcomers. Nevertheless, they were more of a clan than many families. Caleb was the youngest of six sons. All his brothers had married and settled in their valley. All were involved in the shepherding of their landlord's extensive flock of Cheviots.

As Caleb strolled towards the dog kennels, he smiled to himself. He was the next to follow in the family's footsteps and marry a bonnie young lassie. This time next year, Annella will be his lawful wedded wife. Over the summer months, he had spent every spare hour of daylight working on an old, burnt-out crofter's cottage further down the valley. Annella was busy quilting bedspreads and making rag rugs. She had already started jamming fruits and doing all the other things women do to fill their larders with supplies. What a wonderful little lass she was!

"Get moving, man!" Nathan, Caleb's oldest brother, shouted to him, "Dreaming of Annella isn't going to get them sheep down."

"I suppose you're too long married to dream," teased Caleb back.

But Nathan wasn't listening. He was barking orders to his young sons and excited dogs.

"If a mist comes down, you come down," he instructed. "And keep within sight of an adult or Uncle Caleb!"

Caleb sighed. Even though he was now twenty, he would always be the baby boy and could easily outwork Nathan at any job. He longed for his family to take him seriously and treat him like a grown-up. Maybe they would do so once he was married.

Scrambling their way around boulders and along winding sheep tracks, the Baker men slowly climbed their way up the rugged mountainside. The rough gorse and heather scratched their legs as they pushed through overgrown paths. The wind grew stronger, and the chilly air caught in their lungs as the men steadily ascended. Taking a quick breather, they looked back and surveyed Taitneach, their valley. From this height, the whole panorama of it could be seen—from the stately waterfall to the right and the sparkling loch to the far left. Halfway down was a small pass—their doorway to the outside world, the local village, the kirk, and Annella.

From the mountaintop on a clear day, like today, one could see deep into the next glen. Deserted by all but sheep, it lay sad, desolate, and haunting. The ruins of black houses, roofless and decaying, and the pattern of broken stonewalls stood as a stark reminder of the heartbreak the highlanders had received at the hands of their landlords. With grief, bitterness, and anger, the older generation relived the horrors of the highland clearances, or *Fuadaichean nan Gaidheal*, as it was called in Gaelic.

The fiercely independent highlanders had been left in peace for centuries, living in strong family clans ruled by ancient traditions and chiefs, many lawless but some godly. During these centuries, life amongst the mountains almost stood still, each indomitable clan doing what was right in their own eyes, providing for themselves and subduing their enemies as they saw fit. Important to their survival were their equally tough cattle: hardy grazers who were not fussy about what they ate, with long, thick coats making them ideal for the harsh habitat. To the English and Southern Scots, Highlanders were deemed lawless, feudal, and best ignored.

During the long winter evenings, Caleb had heard many Scots discussing the ill-treatment of the highlanders throughout history, from Charlie VI, Bonnie Prince Charlie, to the Jacobite uprising. But although these events had been shocking and bloody, none had touched their particular glen and strath. It was not until forty years ago that Taitneach was touched, and it all came about because of two events far away from the Highlands.

Deep in Kent, England, Lord D'Egerton rejoiced at the birth of his first-born son. Having already sired three daughters, he was relieved to be presented with his heir. With renewed enthusiasm and thoroughness, he examined the accounts of his estates and found them rather disappointing. Far away in Inverness, Factor Alexander Grant, the elderly and benevolent manager of Lord D'Egerton's Scottish estate, decided to retire. A new, enthusiastic manager named Keir was appointed, who, on looking at Grant's accounts, found that the Highland tenants had hardly paid a penny of rent for years. Keir lost no time in arranging a meeting with Lord D'Egerton in London. Lord D'Egerton was reluctant to interrupt his pleasures during the social season in the metropolis, leaving the irritating problem of unpaid rent to Factor Keir.

Drunk with power and wanting to impress his new boss, Factor Keir light-footed back to Scotland and formulated a plan. Thanks to him, the D'Egerton glens would start making money, and the answer was clearly sheep. Not many years before, the Duchess of Sutherland had evicted 15,000 people from their land to make room for 200,000 sheep. That was the future of the D'Egerton estate. Not a man to do things in halves or be outdone by a duchess, Keir engaged the military to execute his project. By now, the dreaded 'redcoats' were experts at terrorising the highlanders, raping their women, plundering their goods, and burning their houses. Nothing was left undone at Taitneach. That day, about two hundred men, women, and children fled their ancestral homes with hardly more than the clothes on their backs.

After living a few days in the wild, most leapt at Factor Keir's cunning offer to cancel their rent debts if they accepted free passage to Ireland. Back in his Inverness office, Keir poured a large whisky and congratulated himself on his remarkable success. All they needed now was an able shepherd. Highlanders were not shepherds but herdsmen, so he wrote to his equal in Kent. Within days, he received the reply he wanted. There was a skilful and ambitious young shepherd on the estate. With a little persuasion and by going scarce on the facts, the young man was enticed by the new adventure, salary, and position. His name was John Baker.

CHAPTER 6

Suzie stood on the cold stone floor, leaning elbow-deep in hot, dirty water. However much she scrubbed the saucepans, she couldn't get rid of all the burnt-on milk. Although tired and cold, she was dripping with sweat, and as it ran down her face, it stung her eyes. Her once-neat bun had long ago yielded to gravity, and lank, greasy strands of hair fell across her face as she leant over the scullery sink. Wearily lifting her red, raw hand to brush them aside yet again, Suzie suppressed a sob that threatened deep within her. *It's no good crying over spilt milk*, her mother had often said, *nor burnt milk*, thought Suzie, using her fingernails to scratch off the stubborn stains. She had already tried using crushed eggshells and lemon, but the acidic mixture had stung her chapped hands so badly that she resorted to her normal fingernail trick.

When the D'Egertons organised a dinner party, they did not consult their scullery maid about what time would suit her. Hours were spent discussing the table settings and flower arrangements, but never, for even the briefest moment, did they consider the washing up. *Do they know what washing up is?* Wondered Suzie. *Probably not.* All day, the kitchens had been the centre of frantic activity. From early dawn, when Suzie lit the great stoves, until late into the evening, when the sweet pastries and lemon sorbet were served, everyone below stairs was in a state of high tension. As the guests finally sipped their coffee, the staff congratulated themselves on a job well done. Slumping themselves down at the kitchen table and taking the weight off their aching feet, the cook's team and footmen tucked into leftovers. The reprieve was short-lived, for Mr Briggs, the Butler, soon arrived and marched the menservants off to clean the glass and silverware.

Suzie had tried in vain all day to keep abreast with the washing up. Time and time again, saucepans, bowls, and utensils were used, cleaned, and then reused. The water geezer huffed and puffed as it reluctantly worked overtime. But the geezer had no reason to complain; it only had one job;

Suzie had hundreds! Everyone needed help; everyone wanted to delegate, and everyone was frantic, so everyone called for Suzie. But now, the kitchens were silent. At 1 am, Mrs Mackie had flung off her apron, declared she would go to bed, and ordered the kitchen maids to do the same. From the depths of the scullery, Suzie wishes the order included herself. Of course, it did not. Some guests were staying over. First thing tomorrow morning, Mrs Mackie expected to step into an immaculate kitchen, ready to start work all over again. There were no kitchen fairies to work their magic, so Suzie would have to execute this transformation single-handed. At half past two, having hung the last pan on its hook and swept the floor, Suzie dampened down the ranges and climbed the stairs to bed. Her every limb ached, and her head pounded as she flopped, fully clothed into bed. In only three and a half hours' time, she would need to light the ranges again. That realisation brought tears of dismay to her eyes. *Don't cry,* she told herself. *It will only waste precious sleeping time.*

Most days were not quite so arduous. Though Suzie hardly had a moment to herself from dawn till dusk, she rather enjoyed being part of the kitchen team. Mrs Mackie worked hard and expected the same from her girls, but she also encouraged and inspired them to try new skills. She saw each of her girls as apprentices and future cooks for the aristocrats. On the other hand, Mrs Benson kept all her professional housekeeping knowledge and deep hidden secrets to enhance her superiority and boss her maids as if they had no gift of independent thought. She spent much of her time lamenting the stupidity of today's maids and wondered where on earth the next generation of good housekeepers (like herself) would come from.

Most of Suzie's days were spent scrubbing pans, peeling potatoes, and plucking games, but every now and again, she was able to help Mabel. On the wonderful days when The Family were dining out and there were only servants to feed, Suzie got to help bake bread and cakes. The kitchen could feel cosy and welcoming on grey winter days. Mrs Mackie scurried around, humming ditties while Kitty, Ruby, and Mabel chatted as they worked. The genial atmosphere seemed to attract the footmen, who gravitated towards the kitchen whenever they could. Mrs Mackie shooed them away if they became too saucy or flirtatious.

"I haven't trained up me lassies just so they can become wives to a wee footman."

"Surely that's their highest ambition, Mrs Mackie," teased the lads.

"In your dreams!" retorted the cook as she chased them with her wooden spoon.

Suzie only saw the other servants at mealtimes. After The Family had been fed, the workforce gathered in the servants' hall for their humble meal. It was far simpler than the elegant food offerings served upstairs, but each meal seemed like a lavish banquet compared to what Suzie was used to at home. If Napoleon Bonaparte believed an army marched on its stomach, Mrs Mackie believed servants worked on theirs too and cooked accordingly. Filling suet puddings, both sweet and savoury, featured regularly on the menu, as did stewed meat, boiled vegetables, and milky porridge. The hard work and long hours made Suzie ravenous, and she happily devoured all she was given with gusto.

But the D'Egertons were not the only ones to be served before Suzie. She and Mabel could not sit down to their plates of lukewarm food until they had served all the servants. At the very top of the table sat the upper servants, or pugs as they were collectively known. Mr Briggs, the Butler, sat at the head of the table and looked every bit the Lord of the Manor. On his right sat the sour Mrs Benson, and opposite her was Mrs Mackie. The rest of the staff sat in rank order down the long tables—valets, footmen, grooms, gardeners, and the garden boy to the right. Ladies' maids, housemaids, and kitchen maids, then Suzie to the left. After Mr Briggs had said an elaborate but insincere grace, the first course was eaten in near silence. Only the upperservants were permitted to speak. Lower servants had to eat in silence unless they were answering an upper servant's question. Mr Briggs enjoyed his food and had a stout figure to testify to the fact, but he also liked the sound of his own voice. The enforced silence permitted him to hold forth uninterrupted.

"I humbly took it upon myself to advise M'Lord this morning that the weather looks unfavourable for riding out. Inclement, I believe, was my choice of words at the time." A mouthful of food disappeared.

"But, if I am not mistaken, he ventured out, notwithstanding." Another mouthful.

"There is a certain, if I might so put it, recklessness about M'Lord at times. A more measured and considered approach to…"

"But it hasn't rained yet, has it?" cut in Mrs Benson curtly. "I don't know what you are fussing about."

"No doubt he had business to attend to," suggested Mrs Mackie.

"But there was dampness in the air, so to speak. One only has to step outside the warm confines of…"

"Kitty, will you stop scraping your knife over your plate like that?" barked Mrs Benson.

Once the pugs had finished their main meal, they stood up. Everyone rose to their feet in respect and remained standing until the upper servants had paraded out of the hall. Immediately the door was shut, the atmosphere relaxed. Now, everyone talked at once; food was flicked, and pranks were played. Ruby served the pugs pudding and coffee in the housekeeper's parlour, while Mabel and Suzie served the rest. The servants' hall resounded with a cacophony of noises as the chairs were pushed back, places swopped, jokes exchanged, and superiors mimicked. One footman was a passable pianist and never lost a minute before hammering out a tune. Others, pudding bowls in hand, joined him around the piano for a sing-song. There was no time to waste because they are aware that a pug or ringing bell could interrupt their enjoyment at any moment. Having more control over their own time, the gardeners and grooms ate their pudding leisurely. Suzie wished she was a gardener and could stop work when darkness fell.

Even when all the other servants were briefly relaxing and having fun, Suzie could not join in. She had to collect the scattered bowl and spoons and start the washing up again. She didn't mind avoiding the noisy footmen, but some of the grooms seemed kind and friendly. Looking after horses was something she knew about from her happy pre-servant days, and she longed to be around animals again or even talk about them. But to her surprise, Suzie was shy in the servants' hall. At school and home, she was always considered a big mouth. But now, she felt timid. Maybe it was her lowly role and position. Perhaps she was too tired to attempt a witty conversation or too scared to tarry long. Maybe it was knowing she looked terrible, with greasy, untidy hair, splattered aprons, and sweaty clothes. The ladies' maids and housemaids all looked so spick-and-span in their smart afternoon uniforms. No one saw the lowly scullery maids, so her uniform lacked all their style and lace. Suzie didn't know what had caused her lack of confidence, but it almost made her cry to think about it.

Apart from her half day off, when she raced home as fast as her legs could carry her, Suzie's only other opportunity to leave the subterranean realm of the kitchen was Sunday morning for the church service. All staff were expected to attend the service, except one of the more senior kitchen maids, who would stay behind to prepare lunch. Suzie was required to either work late on Saturday night or rise early on Sunday morning to peel all the vegetables before the service. Having been schooled to keep the Sabbath from her earliest days, Suzie chose to work late into Saturday evening.

The church intrigued Suzie. There was so much to see, smell, and watch. With candles, incense, and ministers dressed in fine robes, it seemed much more reverent and Old Testament than the plain services she was used to. The choir produced a far superior quality of music than the uncouth blasts of her home congregation. The elegant pipe organ sounded far more genteel than the wheezing old organ, which Mrs Huggins frantically peddled to keep the notes from expiring mid-verse. The acoustics from the beautifully decorated ceiling made the preacher's theatrical voice fill the building with his message. But as she listened to the fine oratory, she realised he actually said very little. With long, carefully chosen and delivered words, he spoke loftily and long about kindness, duty, and thankfulness but nothing about sin or conversion. Suzie was rather pleased with this. All her life, she had heard stirring sermons about sin, death, judgement, and repentance. Every week, she had been urged to turn to Christ. Most Sunday evenings, she had gone to bed, feeling something was amiss. During the week, she could forget about eternity, but on Sundays, the realisation of it looming ahead could no longer be ignored. Right now, she is pleased with a break from all that. She was far too busy, tired, and achy to think about next week, let alone eternity.

CHAPTER 7

Caleb usually rather enjoyed winters—the enforced rest, short days, and storytelling around the fire. However, this year was different. For one thing, it was a far colder winter than they had experienced for many years. The snow started falling in early December and lasted for many weeks. Harsh frosts hardened the drifts, barricading the pass and making the Bakers prisoners in their own strath. For weeks, they had been unable to attend kirk, and he had been unable to visit Annella. As much as he liked his family, he longed to escape their company and predictability. The chill forced them all together around their peat fires. Every evening, his young nephews and nieces gravitated to their grandparents' house, eager to listen to their grandfather's tales of his first years in the Highlands, but Caleb had heard all the stories hundreds of times before.

He knew all about how the alarmed Highlanders had asked their minister to urgently write to Lady Isabel D'Egerton, pleading to let them remain in their settlement. Their faith in her was not misplaced. Dear Lady Isabel Grant had inherited Taitneach, the glen, strath, and surrounding area from her father. On marrying Lord D'Egerton, her inheritance became his property. As a young bride, she had moved south, far away from her beloved Highlands, but always maintained a warm interest in her homeland and its people. Lady Isabel was horrified when she heard of Factor Keir's ruthless evictions and begged her husband to halt the man's barbaric scheme. Lord D'Egerton cared little for 'Philistines' as he called them but respected his wife and marital harmony, so he complied with her wishes. It was too late to save the glen and strath dwellers, but it saved the settlement around the kirk.

Looking through the greyish blue smoke from the smouldering peat fire into the faces of the grandchildren illuminated by its flames, Grandfather Baker continued his story.

"Your grandmother and I had no idea of all these goings on. We expected to be welcomed by other shepherds, but the moment we stepped out of the waggon, we realised there was trouble ahead. We couldn't understand Gaelic, but from one glance at the faces of the people who crowded to meet us, we instantly knew we were not welcome. As we stood at the door of our new cottage, little did we realise its previous inhabitants had recently been thrown out—friends and relatives of the crowd standing around us. Your grandmother was heavily pregnant, and Uncle Nathan was only a wee tot of two years old. We smiled benignly at the mob, but not a single stony face returned our smiles. As an angry man pressed forward, waving a club, wee Nathan cried, and Grandmother fainted. That was just the right thing to do—your granny always knows the right thing to do! The largehearted highlanders couldn't bring themselves to fight such a pathetic little family. One kind woman even ran to fetch some whisky to revive Granny."

The clock ticked on, well past the children's bedtime.

"Go on, Grandfather," they whispered, hoping no one had noticed the time.

"Now, Factor Keir had arranged for us to have a couple of Redcoats (soldiers) for protection. I didn't like the sound of that—it would look like we were expecting trouble. So, I sent them off. I reckon the villagers soon decided I was too young and wet behind the ears to be a threat, and left us alone. It wasan answer to prayer, though. We were mighty grateful when we saw them turn and go home. God looked after us better than a whole army of Redcoats could! Although we didn't understand a word, we went to the kirk every Sabbath. We wanted to meet with the Lord's people, and by their devotion and daily lives, we knew they were God-fearing folks. I'm no scholar, but I made it my business to learn Gaelic. All through that first winter, I studied evening after evening. A kindly old man helped me, patiently correcting my many mistakes. By the spring, I could sing the psalms in Kirk with understanding. Every week, I smiled as I passed by folks, and gradually more were returned. As the flock grew, I needed manpower, and some local men worked for me. Slowly, year by year, bit by bit, your granny and I, and all the family, became accepted."

The said Granny looked up from her knitting.

"Look at the time, children! Caleb, could you find them their coats and distribute them back to their own homes?"

Having delivered his nephews and nieces to their various dwellings on the steading, Caleb crossed the wind-swept yard to the cattle shed, unable to resist the allure of its snugness. The sweet smell of the livestock, the damp warmth of their breath, and the contented sound of their ruminating never failed to bring a smile to his face. He slowly moved his lamp around to survey the beautiful beasts—their shaggy winter coats and long, impressive horns. Peeping at him from behind their long fringes, they cautiously approached, hoping for a handful of oats. Unable to disappoint them, Caleb reached into the food bin.

"Spare a thought for the rest of the herd, ladies," he said as they licked his hands with their long, rough tongues. "Out there in the cold wind, trying to find grass under the snow. Sometimes, it pays to be 'feak and weeble', doesn't it?"

Only the weak and feeble and the three house cows were housed for the winter months. Instead of being just one of the herds, they became friends and pets. The sheep belonged to all the family, but the cattle were Caleb's. When the glen and strath became overgrown with bracken, Caleb had a bright idea. Cattle had roamed the area for centuries, and instead of avoiding bracken, like sheep do, they would trample it down and destroy it. His brothers laughed at his logic, but Caleb used every penny he had and brought a handful of cows in calf. Gradually, his confidence and herd grew, and the bracken and brothers' mocking diminished.

Caleb flopped himself onto a pile of hay with a sigh of satisfaction. With only the restful sounds of the contented cattle around him and the lamp light creating big shadows as it barely penetrated the darkness, Caleb could be alone and pray. Sometimes, he felt closer to heaven in the barn than in the kirk. Here, it was just himself and God. Caleb liked to imagine that the Bethlehem stable was not much different from his Scottish barn, and he rejoiced that his Saviour did not despise a bed of hay.

As well as turning heavenward, Caleb's thoughts wandered to the manse where Annella was still probably toiling away. A few years ago, Taitneach received a new minister with his wife and children. Annella was their maid of all work and came along, too. She was almost part of the ministerial family and enjoyed working for them, but this autumn, she felt slightly disgruntled when the presbytery decided her minister could tutor a student. Now, she had another mouth to feed, room to clean, and a set of white shirts to iron. Caleb smiled. Next year, she would be free from all that and only have his mouth to feed and his shirts to iron.

The days gradually lengthened, and the sunlight felt warmer, turning the hardened snow and soil into stodgy mud. Caleb was determined to battle his way out of the valley and through the treacherous pass as soon as he had an afternoon free to do so. Some sheep had lambed unexpectedly early, creating extra work with very little rewards The lambs needed warming, shelter, and help with feeding, but their chances of surviving were low. Caleb enjoyed lambing, but not this early in the year and not when the work kept him from a trip to Taitneach village.

But Caleb was not the first man to risk the pass. On arriving home, he found a letter waiting for him. Caleb eyed it curiously; the writing looked clumsy and childish. He had never received a letter in all his life. Still booted and hatted, Caleb sat at the kitchen table and read the contents.

Dear Caleb

You will be very surprised to receive a letter from me. Over the long winter months, the ministerial student – Angus, has kindly and patiently taught me my letters. We have developed a strong friendship, and Angus believes I am the woman he should marry. He is a very wise and good man, so he knows what is right. He is sure you will release me from my promise to you when you realise that he has replaced you in my affections. I wish you much happiness on your future pathway.

Yours Sincerely

Annella

Caleb scrunched up the note and, with a roar of anger and anguish, threw it as hard as he could towards the fire. It missed, bounced off the wall, and rolled along the floor. Picking it up again, Caleb read it with disgust— this was not the work of Annella but of Mr Angus Mac-Whatshisname! The religious little hypocrite! Tomorrow, at first light, he would go to the manse and have it out with the man. Caleb would *kindly and patiently* teach him a lesson about stealing another man's fiancée. How could Annella, with all her common sense, prefer a pious, wimpy bookworm to him?

Caleb sank back into his chair. How indeed!? Suddenly, his confidence evaporated. What had he to offer compared with a learned scholar with a bright ministerial future ahead of him? A pastor's wife could wield power in her community. She would be respected, well provided for, and comfortable. All he had to offer was a life of hard graft and uncertain income. He was never going to be anyone special, just the youngest son— belittled and mocked by his big brothers and, from now on, probably pitied. Caleb clenched his fists and closed his eyes tightly. He could stand mocking and give as good as he received, but he could not stand their pity. He would win back his Annella or, or…he wasn't sure. He would not contemplate failure.

The back door quietly opened, and his mother crept into the room, her face pale and drawn but full of sympathy.

"Oh Caleb, I am so, so sorry!" she cried out as she rushed over to hug him.

"How do you know?" he queried gruffly.

"I saw the messenger boy. When he handed over the letter, he told me that Annella and Angus had left for Glasgow together."

"What!?" Caleb shook off his mother's arm and sprang to his feet. "Glasgow!"

"They wanted her parent's blessing for the marriage." Then, as if to appease her son, "The Reverend and his wife are terribly upset and vexed."

Caleb stood still, staring out of the window.

"The whole village is perturbed."

"So, I am the talk of the town," said Caleb in a flat voice, back still to his mother.

"You haven't done anything wrong, my dear. You were wronged."

"How can I show my face there again?"

"I am sure you will only find kindness and sympathy." His mother had moved towards him and laid her hand on his shoulder.

"I don't want kindness and sympathy, Mother. I just want Annella." His voice gave way, and a sob erupted from his chest as he swung around into his mother's embrace.

CHAPTER 8

Lydia hummed to herself as she worked through her morning chores. Today was Suzie's half day, and soon, she would fly through the back door, having run all the way home and breathlessly flung herself into a chair. Having regained her breath, she would talk incessantly about life at the manor for the next few hours.

It was February—the month of waiting. The ground was still too wet and cold to till, and the sheep had another six weeks of pregnancy. The only sign of the long-awaited spring was the increased egg production from the hens and ducks. February could be a dreary, dark month, but Lydia quite liked it. The evenings were gradually becoming lighter, and each tiny sign of spring she would notice over the next few weeks promised new life and a better season than last year. Farmers' wives had to be optimists. Lydia could identify with the Israelite sowers weeping as they scattered their precious seed into the ground, which could have been used to feed their hungry family. It took faith to take wheat from a rapidly dwindling sack of grain and throw it onto inhospitable soil instead of grinding it for flour. Last year, they did not 'return rejoicing, bringing their sheaves with them'. Faith, optimism, and sheer grit were the only things that made them repeat the whole cycle this year.

Over the years, Lydia had worked out something about one's workload—it is unlikely to lessen. Changes happen—parents-in-law die, but these are replaced by other, smaller mouths to feed and bodies to care for. Some work creeps up on you unexpectedly until, before you know it, it becomes a burden you cannot wriggle out of, even if you want to. Take, for instance, Mr Baillie, their neighbour and tenant of Dewbank Farm. After he had lost his wife a few years ago, Lydia took pity on him and took in his washing. From doing his scarce laundry, she started making him the odd pudding. The odd pudding became a daily hot meal. And now, he was almost bedbound, or at least kitchen-bound, and required regular checking. His stove needed feeding, and his water needed drawing. The whole family helped; Matthew chopped up firewood, and the children kept his log basket filled and ran across to check on him. It all took time, and increasingly so. Lydia wondered how they could juggle this extra task in the busy spring and summer months. Yet, had anyone come along and suggested taking over Mr Baillie's care, she would have refused indignantly. Her kindly affection for him had grown as slowly and unperceptively as his vulnerability and neediness. In his care, as in so many other tasks, she missed Suzie's help.

Mr Baillie's sad, hooded eyes always brightened up when they saw Suzie. As well as handing him the prepared meal, she also fed him exciting stories of her work and that of her fellow servants. Enlivened by her enthusiasm, Mr Baillie started to regale stories from his past. Encouraged by Suzie's eager listening, he mixed fact with fiction until he hardly knew what the true facts were himself. Lydia was almost jealous of her daughter's vivacity—she had never sparkled like Suzie, and now she was too tired, old, and careworn. As she peeled the vegetables, Lydia paused and wondered, *'Did Matthew see her like that—old and (what was the opposite to sparkling?)—dull?'* These days, she had little chance to know his opinion on anything. He was too busy hiring himself out of winter pruning of fruit trees. They worked together like well-oiled cogs—efficiently but silently. Was he satisfied with the status quo? She wasn't sure that she was.

"I'm going to London,

London, London.

I'm going to London,

Early next week."

The singing heralded Suzie's arrival. Skipping through the back door, she flung her arms around her mother's waist.

"Mother, I'm going to London!" she beamed.

"So I gather," replied Lydia, wiping her hands dry on her apron and trying to look enthusiastic. "Tell me all about it."

Suzie plonked herself onto a kitchen chair, and Lydia transferred the vegetables from the sink to the kitchen table so she could sit near her.

"Well, the old Dowager lady…."

"Lady Isabel."

"Yes, that's the one.. The townhouse is all 'put to bed' for the winter, and Lord D'Egerton, her son, tries to persuade her not to. But she is going anyway. It is all a bit inconvenient because he is expecting guests, so he does not want to spare the staff. So, it turns out that Kitty (who is terribly bossy) and the awful Mr Briggs (who I think Lord D'Egerton doesn't really like) are going. And I am allowed to go, too. Kitty and Mr Briggs are full of themselves because they have been chosen, but I don't think it is because they are favourites."

Suzie sat and burbled on and on, wondering who would scrub the pots in her absence, laughing at Kitty's airs and graces and Mr Briggs' pomposity. Lydia was still adjusting to the shock of her young daughter going to London. Would she be properly cared for? Had they relinquished their parental rights over her comings and goings by putting her into domestic service?

"Kitty says we won't be busy, just looking after one old lady. Old people don't have big appetites and like plain food. So, we might be able to see something of London. There are public coaches that you can pay to get on." Suzie's tired face beamed with animation. "We could find one going near Buckingham Palace and see where the Queen lives. Kitty says there are lots of concert halls that play beautiful music in the evenings."

"Has Kitty ever been to London?" asked Lydia cautiously.

"Oh no, but several of the footmen have been up there with the family, and they have told us what to do."

Lydia didn't want to be a wet blanket or sour Suzie's half day. She would hold her tongue and see what Matthew had to say.

Flitting from one subject to the next, Suzie ran through her week. "But I am not so sure about the Milton Church now," she commented.

"In what way?"

"I'm not sure that the priest, vicar, or whatever you call him, actually believes the Bible. He drones on about being nice and good, but I don't think he really has anything to offer people."

Lydia nodded encouragingly, hope kindling in her heart.

"I mean, if you were really concerned about your soul and knew your best isn't good enough to get you to heaven, his preaching could leave you frustrated—probably."

Lydia prayed for divine help. Was this the first little shoots of spiritual life in her daughter? Tiny shoots she had been praying for all her daughter's life? But before she could open her mouth to reply, Charlie burst into the kitchen.

"Suzie!" he yelled, jumping on her.

"Charlie-boy!" she answered, wrapping herself around him.

From that moment on, the kitchen was a chaotic cacophony of loud, youthful voices and meal preparations. Elsie wanted to tell Suzie about all the goings on at school, while Charlie badgered his sister to help with the outside chores. Lydia was pleased they were all outside when Matthew returned, so she could tell him about London in private.

"I see," he said, looking grave.

"Can we do anything about it?" Lydia asked.

"Probably not. But I doubt if she will have much time to gad about. Think how hard she normally has to work. It will most likely be the same there."

"But all the awful things that happen in a big city."

"You sound like a right old country bumpkin, Lydia. It can't be that bad."

Yet, another motherly worry crossed Lydia's mind:

"What if she decides she likes the hustle and bustle of London?"

"Our Suzie? She won't; she's a country girl through and through. Look at her now, cuddling the sheep."

Lydia looked and smiled weakly, remaining unconvinced. "Suzie enjoys most things."

"Except school," winked Matthew.

CHAPTER 9

To my dear family:

I hope you are well and hereby send you my love and best wishes. I am in an amazing place in London called Pimlico. It sounds so exotic and un-English, doesn't it? The name makes names like Milton and Brookfield sound very stodgy and dull. You have never seen houses like the ones here. They are all joined together in one long, white row, with an identical, pillared porch and balcony for each house. The ends of the rows are beautifully curved around in a most genteel way that I can't describe. I feared we would be miles away from places like Buckingham Palace, Trafalgar Square, and Hyde Park, but actually, they are all within about two miles. Kitty and I have done lots of walking around and about. We keep to the big roads because the little alleys look confusing and dark. Mr Briggs said that 'Undesirables' lurk in such places, and we were 'by no means' to venture down them. This made us a bit curious, so we disobeyed him and sneaked down one dingy passageway, only to stumble upon a drunkard. We beat a hasty retreat and have since stuck to respectable places where we can see well-to-do children being taken for their daily walks by their governesses or nursery maids. And don't worry, we never go out after dark. We can only explore the area once our morning chores are done and before we need to prepare the evening meal.

I am seeing quite a lot of Lady Isabel, and I think she is a really sweet old lady. I am here to do all the jobs no one else likes to do, like emptying the chamber pots, lighting the fires, peeling the vegetables, and plucking the poultry. Lady Isabel has her own lady's maid, who is almost as ancient as herself. Between them, they speak a strange, throaty language, which Mr Briggs says is Gaelic. When they speak normal English, their accent is so melodious and soft that it sounds very friendly. Mr Briggs says that after all these years, it is a terrible shame that Lady Isabel persists in stubbornly clinging to her Scottish roots, but I like it and think it isn't his place to say these things. I can hardly stand Mr Briggs. In Lady Isabel's presence, he is a picture of politeness and respect, but down in the kitchen, when he knows it is only Kitty and I listening, he is so rude about her, calling her a silly old bat. I really do not trust him.

A few days have passed since I wrote my last sentence. The bell rang, and I had to go. Lady Isabel decided the weather was crisp and sunny enough for a daily constitutional. A strange, wheeled chair was dragged out of some storeroom, and I was given the task of pushing her along the streets to a towpath along the Thames. I thought a responsible job like that would be given to her maid or Mr Briggs, but her maid has lumbago, and Mr Briggs seems to think it is beneath him. He thinks most jobs are beneath him. At first, I was really annoyed about having my afternoons wrecked by Mr Briggs's delegation, but now I am really pleased with the arrangement. Lady Isabel is wrapped up warm in a Scottish blanket and directs me where to go.

The chair is heavy and awkward, but I think it is fairly stable. Once we reach her desired destination, she instructs me to sit on a bench next to her, and we watch the goings on. If we are near the Thames, we watch the boats. If we are in a park, we watch the trees swaying, children playing, and passersby. Then, from the depths of her blankets, she starts talking. I am unsure if she is talking mainly to me or herself, but it is so interesting, and her voice is so melodious. I don't understand half of it, but she talks about the past and her beloved Highlands of Scotland. It all sounds wonderful. Her accent thickens as she remembers her younger days and the folks she used to know, and her voice fills with longing. Every now and again, she seems to remember I am there and says, with a sigh, "Aach, but Ye ne'er knew thaim". I hardly say a word. I want to ask her so many questions, but it would be rude and impertinent. When she starts feeling cold, we head home and go from the past to the present. Every day, I get more fond of her, and that makes me dislike the stuck-up Mr Briggs even more.

I had better go, as it will soon be time for today's walk.

With much love from your devoted daughter (and sister),

Suzie

P.S. I have to smile when I think that a country bumpkin like me is treading the streets of London with a Lady and that Miss Mapel has never been here.

From the moment Mr Briggs proudly pocketed the house keys presented to him by the dowager, Suzie felt a quiver of misgivings. Handing over a heavy ring of keys was the ultimate sign of trust. As the days passed, the misgivings gradually evolved into alarm. At first, Briggs surreptitiously visited the wine cellar and lingered there, but he became brazen as the days passed. Once he realised that Lady Isabel's maid never entered the servant's hall, he began drinking openly there. His mood turned belligerent as he wielded his power over Kitty and Suzie. *If they dared breathe a word about his use of his employer's bountiful generosity towards him to anyone else, he knew how to make their lives a misery. Did he make himself clear?* Suzie trembled as she looked into his piercing, bloodshot eyes and silently nodded to him. Yes, she understood. In the privacy of their attic bedroom, Suzie was more vocal.

"How dare that vile, bad-breathed man get away with daylight robbery? We must do something!"

Kitty sat up in bed and hugged her knees.

"Suzie, I beg of you, don't do anything you live to regret."

"I would live to regret not standing up to the odious man!"

"Have you ever, in your sheltered life, had to deal with a drunk?"

"No!" Suzie felt startled by Kitty's unusually serious tone.

"My father was one and knew how to make our lives as miserable as possible."

"Oh, Kitty, I am so sorry. I never realised," started Suzie, not knowing what to say to her friend.

"Of course, you didn't realise. It isn't something I ever speak about. I don't want to even think about it."

Suzie quietly sat down on her bed. Anything she said now would sound crass. Words were too limiting. It was Kitty who broke the heavy silence.

"He beat us black and blue for the slightest reason, then cried for forgiveness, only to do it again another night. He drank up all our money long before payday. He always had excuses; he always saw himself as the victim. He threatened and scared my mother until she was a nervous wreck. Only her love for us kept her alive."

"You are talking in the past tense." Suzie gently probed, "Is he... Is he...?"

"He is dead," stated Kitty bluntly. "Drink killed him. Sometimes, we wouldn't see him for days. He would sleep rough. One winter's night, he must have fallen asleep and frozen to death."

Suzie could hardly contemplate the awfulness of the situation—to be drunk to oblivion, then suddenly awake on the other side of death, before one's Creator, having full, un-earthly clarity about your eternal destiny—too late. She shivered.

"Is your mum alive?" she asked.

"Yes, she is alive and finally flourishing, but I don't think she will ever be able to really trust a man again."

Suzie wondered if Kitty could ever trust a man either. The father may have died, but the hurt lived on. As they settled down to sleep, the question that Suzie really wanted to ask kept going around in her head: *"Did Kitty's mother, and even Kitty herself, know anything of the Heavenly Father's love?"* Hurting people like them needed to know. She prayed for them. Did she know His love? She knew enough about it to long for it. As she drifted off to sleep, she heard the beautiful sound of Lady Isabel and her maid singing an evening psalm. Their aged voices were shrill rather than sweet, and their merging voices clashed on quivering notes, yet the wabbling sound intensified the muddled but deep desires in Suzie's heart. Believing should be so easy, so why did she find it so hard?

CHAPTER 10

The following afternoon's walk was cut short by inclement weather. As the grey clouds thickened and the wind blew up, Suzie scurried along the pavement, pushing the heavy bath chair as fast as possible. Her feeling of triumph that she had made it home without overturning the whole thing and depositing the dowager quickly evaporated when Mr Briggs and the lady's maid rushed to the door, bundled their employer inside, and looked at Suzie as if the weather was all her fault. In the kitchen, Kitty seemed no less petulant, grumbling that Suzie's walks left her to do all the work. Feeling as if she could please no one, Suzie discarded her coat, donned her apron, and got busy peeling potatoes. *A nice cup of tea would go down well,* she thought wistfully.

Rain lashed against the kitchen windows, and nightfall came early. The mood in the kitchen mellowed, and the room began to feel cosy. Mr Briggs went upstairs to do a job he did not deem beneath him—lighting the gas lamps. How he prided himself on his masterly management of the dangerous contraptions! Only he could be trusted to trim the wicks and switch on the gas in such a way as to produce an evenly burning light and avoid causing a tragic explosion. While he was away, Kitty and Suzie crept out of the kitchen into the servants' hall and examined his latest acquisition from the cellar.

"How dare he!" exclaimed Kitty.

She and Suzie studied the half-empty bottle.

"The cheek of it!"

"What is it?" asked Suzie, ignorant of all things stronger than tea.

"He is drinking whisky from the family's own secret distillery in Scotland."

Suzie did not know what a distillery was, but it sounded particularly impertinent to drink something homemade. She could stand by no longer!

Upstairs in her parlour, Lady Isabel was entertaining a dear old friend, Lady Livesey. Their friendship went back many years and was founded on common values and uprightness. In the murky world of high society, Lady Livesey stood out as a beacon of decency, integrity, and respectability. Lady Isabel aspired to imitate her friend. She normally came flying the (metaphorical) flag of some new noble cause she had embraced, and tonight's visit was no exception.

"My dear Isabel, intoxicating drinks are the curse of the working class, the nails in many a coffin, and the shame of the gentry. We, in influential positions, all need to sign the pledge of abstinence."

Lady Isabel signed inwardly. She was prepared to throw money at any of her friend's worthy projects. She was very used to that, but signing the pledge? Surely, this was pushing the friendship just a little too far. Lady Livesey seemed rather intoxicated with her own verbosity. It could prove to be a long and tiring evening. Lady Isabel busied herself with the teapot, playing for time. She had just balanced the tea strainer on her cup for a refill when the door burst open, and Suzie rushed in.

"My lady, Mr Briggs, is drinking your own special whisky from your own distillery!"

Lady Isabel lost grip of the bone china teapot. It hit the table heavily; the lid bounced off and smashed on the floor. Lady Livesey's mouthful of tea erupted out of her lips and showered the embroidered tablecloth and buttered teacakes. Suzie let out a strangled scream at the chaos she had created.

Into this scene of parlour pandemonium marched Mr Briggs, a figure of composure and control.

"Did I hear unrest, M'Lady?"

"I am so sorry, I never realised you were entertaining a...." blabbered Suzie, but she was silenced by a wave of Briggs's hand.

"I apologise for the rude interruption of your tea party, M'Lady," fawned Briggs. "This young girl fills her pretty little head with far too many dramatic novelettes."

"Please remove her from my presence, Briggs," replied Lady Isabel in a tremulous voice. "And send for my smelling salts. And my dear guest's carriage."

"Of course, M'Lady. And shall I ask the girl to pack her bags forthwith?"

Lady Isabel waved a dismissive hand towards the door. "Do as you wish, Briggs. Do as you wish."

Having been frogmarched out of the parlour and to the servants' hall, Suzie sank into a chair and cried. Was this really happening? Had Lady Isabel really given Briggs the power to dismiss her instantly? Briggs left her in no doubt about the answer.

"Get upstairs, girl. Pack your bags and leave the premises. Ya first job in the big wide world didn't last long, did it?"

Kitty stood at the door, wringing her apron in her hands. "But sir, it is dark. You can't let a girl roam London alone in the dark; it isn't safe."

"She should have thought about that before she tried snitching on me, shouldn't she?"

He shoved his red face into Suzie's, overpowering her with his whisky breath. "That'll teach ya not to meddle with me—move it!"

Suzie ran upstairs and packed in a dazed hurry. Almost nothing belonged to her, she realised. Even the clothes she was wearing belonged to her employer. She fumbled at the buttons and changed into the only set of clothes she owned. Her mind was too panicked to think straight. All she could do was sob, "Lord, help me," over and over again.

Having dressed up warmly, Suzie reluctantly made her way downstairs to the back door. The stony-faced Briggs and weeping Kitty were waiting. Briggs tried to shove her out the door, but Kitty got in first and briefly hugged and kissed her. The girls sobbed on each other's shoulders until they were wrenched apart by Briggs. Just as she was leaving, Suzie felt Kitty slip something into her hand and heard her whisper, "Go there." The next moment, the door was slammed shut and bolted behind her, and she was all alone in the darkness and driving rain.

CHAPTER 11

Suzie stumbled along the cobbled, slippery pavement, hurrying to—she knew not where. The hissing streetlamps, giving a flickering and uncertain light, became her focus. Looking skyward, she could detect no break in the clouds—the moon would be useless to her tonight. She would follow the lamps until they led her to a brighter, more sheltered place where she could read Kitty's note. Suzie's imagination ran riot as she fought a rising panic. Everyone had sinister stories to tell about London at night—the gangs, drunken rough sleepers, and evil men stalking the streets to attack lone females. Hunger and dread twisted in her stomach. On and on, she scurried away from familiar roads and into the unknown. A sudden screech behind her sent her heart leaping to her throat—it was a couple of cats fighting.

Suzie pulled her woollen shawl over her head and soggy bonnet and steeled herself. It wasn't really nighttime yet, and this was a respectable area. She needed to be sensible and controlled. Praying "Lord, please help me" for the hundredth time, she willed her shaky legs to keep walking. Away from the residential streets, the pavements were busier. There were a few ladies but many men. Suzie hugged her bag closer and slipped her shawl down to her shoulders. *Forget trying to save the bonnet. I need to know what is happening on either side of me.* Turning a corner, Suzie spied just the sort of thing she was looking for—a smart hotel with a well-lit pillared porch—and no footmen standing guard! A tiny ray of hope dawned as she escaped the rain and sat on the wide doorstep. Unfolding Kitty's crumpled note, she let out a cry of dismay and despair! The rain, or her sweaty palm, had caused the ink to smudge and stain her hand. Not a word was readable. Suzie's head sank to her knees, and she sobbed.

In her distress, she did not see the elegant footman opening the hotel door or his look of disdain. All she knew was the sharp kick of his polished shoe on her thigh.

"Get away with ya!" he commanded, "One of our guests is exiting."

Suzie jumped out of the way. Through her tears, she could see a handsome couple in the foyer being helped into their coats. The hotel looked so warm, dry, and inviting, and the pair looked so happy.

"Be off with you!" The footman snarled and waved his hand impatiently at Suzie before opening the door for the guests with a bow and an ingratiating smile.

Suzie just wanted to crumple into a heap, but her tired legs plodded onward. Her dress, saturated with rain, clung heavily to her, making each step harder. A dark spire came into view against the night sky. At first, she thought it was a church, but on seeing a twin spire near it, Suzie realised they weren't spires but the towers of a suspension bridge over the Thames. Her geographical knowledge of the area beyond her daytime walks was very sketchy. Still, Suzie remembered Briggs scoffing at the fact that Pimlico Train Terminus was not in Pimlico but over the river on the south bank. There and then, Suzie decided that was where she would go. Surely, there would be light, shelter, and a kindly station master there.

Suzie was dismayed to discover that she needed to pay a toll. Deeply hidden in her carpet bag was a little drawstring purse holding a few coins. Escaping out of the fast-moving bridge queue, Suzie sided up to the toll booth wall and cautiously rummaged in her bag as if it contained the crown jewels. Finally, clutching a penny, she re-joined the queue and paid the toll.

At the midpoint of the bridge, Suzie stopped to admire the view. Through a slight break in the clouds, a full moon shone. Below her, the wide river, glistening in the moonlight, was still busy with boats of all shapes and sizes transporting goods to and from the docks. Lights flickered out from many little portholes—tantalising peeps into a very different life, wetting her curiosity. The wind hummed tunefully as it rushed through the railings and suspension cables. The cool blast on her face and the beguiling scene exhilarated Suzie. Maybe it was her imagination, but the bridge beneath her seemed to sway. This was the nearest she had ever been to being on a boat at sea. She closed her eyes and imagined standing at the helm of a ship voyaging its way to uncharted territories. Not so very far from the truth, she realised. Remembering that she was still clutching the useless note, Suzie lifted her hand and opened her palm, allowing the paper to fly on the wind and dance down and down to the murky waters. Looking up at the moon-lit sky, Suzie silently quoted Psalm 121:

I to the hills will lift mine eyes,

from whence doth come mine aid.

My safety cometh from the Lord,

who heav'n and earth hath made.

The rain clouds once again eclipsed the moon, and Suzie resumed her walk, but now, instead of total despair and panic, she felt a tiny ray of hope and peace. She needed to trust in the God of her parents.

The train station was well-lit, easy to find, and had, oh, the luxury of a water closet! The entrance seemed full of people who, unlike her, knew where they were going and had an air of purpose. Unable to decide her next move, Suzie sat on a bench and thought. Once again, she cautiously delved into her bag, found her purse, and counted her coins. A cloud of gloom descended when she discovered she only had a sixpence left. Definitely not enough for a train fare to Milford! Maybe her parents' God was not as interested in her as He was in them. But having no one else to turn to, she continued her repeated prayer for help. Suzie stared vacantly at the comings and goings.

Businessmen running to catch the last train home, porters unloading trunks and boxes, and arrivals being greeted by family. A kindly, white-haired man caught her attention as he stepped out of a carriage. He looked like a visiting minister from her chapel in Brookfield—the sort of preacher who speaks simply and includes the children. Her first impulse was to approach him and ask for help, but on second thoughts, it seemed inappropriate and rash. *Don't judge a book by its cover, Suzie,* she warned herself as she watched him disappear through an arch and into the night. But the sight of him helped her formulate a new plan. The safest people to approach are chapel people. Chapel people will be found in a chapel tomorrow, so to a chapel she would go. But first, she had to see out the night. Her stomach grumbled, reminding her that her last meal was a very long time ago. A coffee stall owner was still serving the late travellers, and after much deliberation, Suzie decided to spend two pence on a cup of tea and a currant bun. This only left her with four pence, but she needed to keep her energy up to search for a chapel, so it seemed worth it.

A church bell struck eleven o'clock. It was going to be a long night on the hard bench. Suzie thought she would look conspicuous as she laid down on it, so she put her bag as a pillow on the armrest and sat, leaning her head against it. She closed her eyes.

"Hey, you!" Suzie felt a prod, "You can't stay here; the station is closing."

A large porter towered over her.

"But where can I go?" whimpered Suzie at the end of her tether.

The porter did not look nasty, but as if any sympathy for the homeless had drained away long ago.

"Under them arches is the normal place," he said, pointing to the back exit.

Like a criminal to the gallows, Suzie plodded in the direction she had been shown. Just outside the soon-to-close gates of the station was a whole cluster of downtrodden humanity. Suzie shrank back when she saw them. Many were already asleep; some were sitting against the arches, drinking or smoking, and a few more were gathered around a lamp, playing cards. At her approach, a couple of men raised their drink bottles and leered at her.

"Ya leave,'er alone, ya vagabonds," screeched a toothless old woman, and the men immediately stopped.

"Come 'ere to me wiv a cuppa tea 'n' a bit te eat, en I'll look after ya, gal." Suzie looked at the hard, shrewd face and realised this was the best offer she would get that evening. Anyway, it probably wouldn't pay to fall out with a matriarch like that. Hurrying back to the coffee stall before it closed, Suzie bought the insurance gift, returned to the old hag, and tentatively sat beside her. The scalding tea and currant bun disappeared with the rapidity of a fully toothed and iron-throated individual. The woman then wiped her hairy chin with a grubby hand, let out a satisfied belch, and laid down to sleep. Curling up and wrapping herself in her sodden cloak, Suzie tried to do likewise. Using her precious bag again as a pillow and pulling the cloak over her head, Suzie tried to cocoon herself from her surroundings. The sights could be shut out, but not the smells. Unwashed bodies, urine puddles, alcohol breath from wide-sleeping mouths, and tobacco smoke combined to produce a nauseating stench. The stone floor was hard and cold, but Suzie dared not move and disturb her protector.

As she lay cold, damp, and uncomfortable, the same old nagging concern came back to her as it did every night. She had no problems believing that God had the power to save her. She knew He was Almighty, but was He willing to? This uncertainty robbed her of any joy in trusting. He willingly saved her parents, but her? She thought that some of her prayers had been heard that night. After all, she was still alive and well, but what if they hadn't gone beyond her skull?

The trains blowing off steam woke Suzie with a start. She couldn't believe that she had actually slept. Turning over, she discovered that the old woman had left already. Getting up stiffly, Suzie shook off her shawl, straightened her skirts, and made her way to the ladies' room. It was refreshing to splash her face with cold water and drink a little from her cupped hands. She just had enough money for a cup of tea and a currant bun. Was it breaking the Sabbath to buy a small breakfast? Suzie decided it was like the disciples gathering the grains of a few ears of wheat from the field—a necessity. Suzie hunted in her bag for her purse but couldn't find it anywhere. She sat on a bench to have a thorough investigation, but to no avail. It had definitely gone along with her ivory comb and small-looking glass. Indignantly, she wondered how the toothless old crone had managed to purloin them from a bag she had clung to all night. Despite her irritation and rumbling tummy, she had to admire the skill.

Feeling grubby, dishevelled, and hungry, Suzie left the station's shelter and headed onto the quiet streets. A church clock struck seven. Being a Sunday, there was not the normal bustle of early morning deliveries, tradesmen, and street cleaners, but at least, it was starting to get light, and the rain had stopped. Finding a chapel is easier said than done. Churches were easy, as one could hear the bells and look for spires, but chapels were silent, and their roofs just blended in with the surroundings. Several times, she spied something in the distance and trudged towards it, only to find it was a Quaker meeting house, Working Men's Mission, or the like. As the pavement filled, she tried another method, but following people was no good either. Suzie found that she couldn't tell the difference between a Roman Catholic, Anglican, or Nonconformist by their outward appearance. By now, her feet were blistered, and her strength was waning.

Finally, she found herself outside a modest brick building, sitting behind a wrought iron fence. Over the front door was the name 'Bethesda'. This would do; she could hardly go a step further anyway. Once behind the iron fence, Suzie hesitated. *"I must look like a scarecrow!"* she thought. She took off her crushed bonnet, tried to smooth her hair, adjusted her hair pins, and replaced her hat. Wishing she could be invisible, she headed towards the entrance. Much to her relief, the doorman was so busy having a hushed chat with a couple heading for the left door of the lobby that she could sneak in through the right one. Hardly daring to look up, she spied an empty pew at the back and slid into it.

The chapel's interior seemed so familiar that Suzie felt a wave of homesickness sweep over her. The beautifully polished wooden panelling went up to shoulder height, and the large windows were cleverly positioned to let the sunlight in without giving a view of what was going on outside. Theere were rows of wooden pews with little shelves for hymn books and Bibles. The congregation seemed a step up from the Brookfield people. They were far more elegant, stylish, and grand. Suzie felt even more bedraggled.

The service was simple and good, but Suzie could not concentrate. Her stomach was protesting, her feet were throbbing, and her mind was darting from one worry to another. A little boy in the pew in front of her turned and stared at her, then pinched his nose. Her dress and cloak had started emitting the odours they had collected overnight. Suzie determinedly ignored him and held her head high, but inwardly, she shrivelled with embarrassment. The minister looked and spoke like a kindly grandfather. Suzie hoped it would be him and not some harsh deacon who dealt with her later.

Sitting through the service was the easy bit, but sitting still afterwards as the building gradually emptied was much harder. Suzie studiously stared at a hymnbook on her lap as the congregation filed out.

The caretaker, whose mind was already on his Sunday dinner, strutted up to Suzie.

"It's time you went, Missy. I'm about to lock up."

"But I've nowhere to go. I need some help, please." Suzie's anxious eyes filled with tears.

"Well, I am about to lock up."

"I've got nowhere to go," wailed Suzie, bursting into tears.

In his mind's eye, the dinner was cooling and congealing. "I need to lock up," he insisted.

"What is all this about?" asked an authoritative female voice. Looking up, Suzie saw a plump, grey-haired lady sailing up the aisle.

"We've got a homeless person situation," explained the caretaker, pointing at Suzie with his keys.

"I'm not homeless! And I am not a situation!" insisted Suzie, "but I do need help. Please!"

The lady reached for the keys, "I can lock up; thank you, Mr Barrow," she said, watching him leave the building before sitting down next to Suzie.

"Now, my dear, please explain your predicament."

CHAPTER 12

All through lambing, Caleb worked as if his life depended on it, and it felt like it did. He did not want time to sit and stew. He did not want time to socialise or lay awake in bed with his depressing ruminations, so he worked himself to exhaustion, hoping to earn some deep, thought-obliterating sleep. Ever since receiving the letter from Annella, Caleb had avoided Taitneach village as much as possible. He attended kirk on Sundays but rushed off as soon as the final 'Amen' had been uttered. The sheep were an excellent and plausible excuse for bolting back to the barns, but lambing does not go on forever.

Everyone had been kind, but even that was hard to bear. He did not want his brothers, sisters-in-law, and parents tip-toeing around him all the time. He missed being teased and ridiculed. He was indignant about Annella but did not want to hear others condemning her. It was the po-faced Angus he felt so mad with. He imagined some pale, thin, bespectacled weed of a man. Poor Annella was hitched up with someone who didn't appreciate her humour, cheeriness, and bounce. Maybe those lovely traits had already been sapped from her. Caleb couldn't bear the thought of her being downtrodden, patronised, or ill-used. Sometimes, he took his frustrations out on the log pile.

Chopping logs became therapeutic, but as he welded the axe with all his pent-up might, he alarmed himself at his own strength and anger. Hating a man is always wrong, even if he has run off with your fiancée. He didn't want to become a bitter and twisted person. He had to believe God knew what He was doing, even if it didn't feel like it. He had to believe "all things work together for good to them that fear the Lord," even though he couldn't imagine how. Some days, it felt as if his faith was only just clinging to God by the skin of its teeth. It would have been easier to give up and sink into a downward spiral of atheistic depression. *Don't listen to yourself, but talk to yourself,* he reasoned. Quote Bible promises and make yourself listen.

As the days began to lengthen and warm and the ewe and lambs were moved up to the high pasture, a plan began to take root in Caleb's mind. He had always loved Taitneach, the family's valley, and their private little kingdom. He loved the majestic scenery, the changing moods of the mountains and waterfalls from season to season, and the rhythm of the farming year. Being cut off from the outside world, most winters had always felt embracing and cosy. Being self-sufficient as a big family clan through the hard, cold months was a way of life he loved, and they all prided themselves in. It was just them against the raw, unpredictable elements that yearly challenged their survival. Most of the summer's activities were preparations for winter survival—making hay, pickling, preserving, and repairing.

"A penny for your thoughts, lad." His father's comment interrupted his musings. It was one of those rare evenings when there were no grandchildren visiting—just him and his parents around the fire.

Caleb wanted to brush off the question with a glib answer, but he couldn't keep avoiding the subject. He looked into his Pa's eyes and saw tender concern. They deserved to understand his broodings, but it may well hurt them, which is why he had put it off for so long.

"I've been thinking about my future." His Ma looked up and put down her knitting. Picking up a stick to be used for kindling, Caleb started whittling it with his pen knife and continued.

"Had I married Annella and been living in an old crofter's cottage, I would never have wanted to leave Taitneach. But really, this valley is too small to sustain all our families, especially as our tribe keeps growing." Caleb shaved more and more bark off the twig. "I am never going to rise up the pecking order. I will always be the baby brother, and now I am the jilted baby brother." He stopped himself; he did not want to sound sour. He didn't want to tell them that the ghost of his happy courting days lingered in every nook and cranny of the valley.

"So, what is your plan?" prompted his Pa.

Taking a big breath in and carving carefully, Caleb explained, "I need to get away for a while, be my own boss, and plough my own farrow."

He looked up at his parents. It hit him that they weren't getting any younger. A great burst of protective love for them almost engulfed him and drowned out any ambition he had.

"You're right, my lad." Relief at his father's reply perked Caleb up again. "You need to get away from here for a bit. You've got a good business head on you. Look at your success with cattle, and you know how to graft."

56

"Brain and brawn," added his mother.

"Aay, just that."

Caleb felt humbled by the rare, high praise. "I don't know if I will make much of a go at it, but as a bachelor, I'm not responsible for anyone else, so I can give it my best shot."

"Remember, Caleb, your mother and I upped sticks and came right up here from down south, so we know a bit about branching out."

Caleb smiled; his brothers hadn't even moved a mile, but his game-old parents had really been adventurous in their younger days.

"But where are you planning to go?" asked his mum anxiously. "Not Canada, are you?"

"Oh no!" replied Caleb quickly, "I don't know where, but somewhere closer than that. But maybe somewhere with a milder climate to try cereal and maybe fruit farming."

He put down his whittling and continued animatedly, "I want to rent a small holding or farm for a bit. I will sell my cattle to fund it. I couldn't move them away from here anyway. If I find I don't like the area, I can give up the tenancy after a couple of years and look for another place. I want to be fairly near a train station so that maybe some of you will come and visit once in a while. I'll take my dog so as to have a sensible being to talk to of an evening."

"I'll send you hampers of preserves, pickles, and the likes," offered Ma.

"So, you don't think I'm mad, reckless, or anything?" asked Caleb.

"How could I accuse you of that?" laughed Pa. "I wasn't much older than you when I took my young wife – "

"– heavy with child," butted in the said wife.

"Aay, heavy with child and a wee little toddler, from civilised Kent, right up North, far away from friends and family."

"And against your parents-in-law's wishes."

"Aay, against their very strongly expressed wishes!" The couple grinned at each other, sharing the memory. "So, in short, how can I call you reckless?"

"We're going to miss you, Caleb dear." His mother looked tenderly at her lastborn and said, "But we don't want you just moping about here. Going is the right thing for you."

"Have I been moping about? I would call what I have been up to 'lambing.'"

"Aay, you've worked extremely hard, but you've lost your sparkle."

Caleb wasn't quite sure what his sparkle was, but he knew he had lost something important.

"But I am not sure how to find tenancy."

His father threw a log on the fire and thought for a while. "I'll make enquiries with the D'Egerton's factor. They have small tenancies all over the place."

CHAPTER 13

By the time lambing had ended, Lydia realised she had lost two important men in her life. Mr Baillie went to sleep one evening, never to awake. This should not have shocked her—every morning, she went over with porridge for him and wondered what she would find. But it knocked her more than she had imagined when it actually happened. She was sad that the poor old man had died alone. She felt guilty that she hadn't spent more time with him (though how she could have found the time without adding more hours to a day, she wasn't sure). She felt guilty that she hadn't spoken more of the gospel to him. She felt guilty for being slightly relieved that there was one less responsibility on her shoulders.

The other loss was far less obvious; sometimes, she wondered if it was all in her imagination. It was Matthew. He was still very much there in person. He still worked every daylight hour. He still ate every meal set before him and faithfully fulfilled all his responsibilities. Yet, it was all done in a gloomy silence, unlike his normal self. Matthew had never been the life and soul of any party. He was more likely to laugh at a joke than to crack one. He had always preferred his vegetable patch to a social event any day. But this was different; maybe he was just fed up with her. Perhaps it was all her fault for not giving him enough support or admiration. Men need female admiration to feel loved, don't they? Maybe she had taken him too much for granted. Whatever the cause was, Matthew was melancholy and (she hated to admit it to herself) a bit sour and selfish.

She wanted to be supportive and sensitive, but actually, she felt a bit resentful. They had all been through a tough year; life on the farm was hard work. He hadn't had the extra burden of looking after Mr Baillie to deal with. Why should she always have to be the little ray of sunshine in the household? Jollying people along for the sake of a harmonious family life was not as easy as it looked. It should be the responsibility of every grown-up adult for the common good.

Now, she woke up every morning wondering what mood Matthew would be in. If he was cheery, she wondered how long it would last. A small, trifling matter, like Charlie knocking over his water glass at the table, could spark an outburst, and the gloom and irritation could last all day, with them all tiptoeing around him. If it were Charlie acting this way, she would have sat him down and explained how such behaviour is unacceptable. But you can't really do that to your husband. Matthew didn't seem to like her, Charlie, or Elsie's company anymore, and he certainly didn't like himself.

Lydia wished she could chat with some wise old friend about the situation. But that was impossible for a few reasons. Over the last decade, she had been too busy to have a deep friendship with other women. She had never felt the need to. Normally, she chatted with Matthew about her problems. Anyway, even if she had a close friend, talking about Matthew would seem disloyal. She still loved him and did not want anyone to think less of him. He was a good, kind man, and she needed to keep giving. It was Saturday morning, and Matthew was banking up his rows of potato plants. She took him out a cup of tea, and they sat together on a pair of upturned logs, having a well-earned break. The apple blossom was fully out, looking beautiful against the blue sky. Lydia wrapped her arm around her husband's far shoulder and lean her head on him as she drank in the pleasant scene and felt the warm sun on her face.

"What a beautiful day!" she cooed.

"Umm!"

"The sun is really getting warmer."

Silence.

"Elsie is picking up pastry making and progressing really well. Today, she is busy trying rough puff." If Matthew still liked anyone, it was Elsie.

"Good," he replied distractedly. He was watching Charlie chop logs. "He isn't handling the axe correctly—again!"

Lydia removed her arm and head from him. Charlie could be very annoying. She had to admit it, but Matthew hadn't a good word to say about him these days.

"Maybe you could give him a lesson," she tentatively suggested. Spending time together on a project would do them both good.

"'Maybe you could do this; maybe you could do that!'" mimicked Matthew. "Do I look as if I am twiddling my thumbs?" And with that, he stood up, threw his dregs of tea on the grass, and marched off. Lydia's shoulder muscles tightened into a knot. Such knots, she had discovered, lasted all day and often led to headaches. *Probably my fault again.*

The rest of the day would have looked idyllic to a casual observer. The sun continued to shine. Elsie's pastry became a delicious chicken pie, and they had a bonfire of all Mr Baillie's unusable old bedding and clothes. Everyone likes a good bonfire! But underneath, there was a layer of energy-sapping tension. Charlie was rebuked for prodding the fire too much and then for not attending to the fire. He was told off for eating with his mouth open, slurping his drink, and scrapping his chair. Elsie sat silently with big eyes. Sometimes, she looked meaningfully at Charlie, trying to convey a warning against walking into trouble, but her signals were not heeded or understood. Charlie's behaviour was irritating, but choosing which parental battles to fight and which to leave was an art Matthew had (hopefully, temporarily) lost.

Lydia enjoyed Sunday evenings. They all gathered around the roaring stove with warm milk and a biscuit, and Matthew read the family a good, tear-jerking Christian story. However hard up they were, Lydia always managed to find something sweet as a Sunday treat. Elsie would curl up in the rocking chair, and Charlie would lay on the hearth rug, playing with his wooden Noah's ark. Having sat through Sunday school and two long services, Charlie would be a bit restless and provoking. Usually, they had an afternoon walk between the services to get off some energy, but today had been too rainy. Despite the weather, Lydia wished that Matthew had put on his coat and taken Charlie. Maybe she should have. Instead, they both had a nap.

The evening started with cosy promise. The story was suitable, sad, and moving. There was enough sugar to stir a little into the hot milk, and the biscuits were still fresh.

Matthew began reading, "The harsh north wind blew mercilessly through the draughty garret, and the poor, hungry children clung together under their thin, moth-eaten blanket. The candle their mother had left had long since flickered out and…"

Bang, bang! Charlie's queue of animals awaiting admission into the ark began to fight. The lions were attacking the bears.

"Charlie, stop that now! Why can't you just listen for a change?" roared Matthew.

"I am listening."

"Then what is the story about?"

"Orphans?"

"NO! I knew you weren't listening."

"It's usually about orphans," insisted Charlie, "and they normally die young."

Lydia couldn't help smirking at this apt summary. Matthew happened to catch the amusement, and it annoyed him even more.

"You're too old to play with little toys, Charlie. Sit on a chair like the rest of us."

He wasn't too young last week, thought Lydia. "Charlie, why not come and sit on my knee and listen quietly?"

"No, he will not!" insisted Matthew. "He can sit on his own chair and listen quietly. Or is that too much to ask? And Elsie, will you stop rocking that silly chair? You'll end up crashing into the bookcase!"

Crestfallen, Elsie stopped immediately. Charlie rose to his feet and walked towards the chair, kicking the ark over as he went.

THUMP!

Matthew threw the book on the floor.

"Get to bed now, before I give you a hiding!" he shouted.

Charlie looked like a scared rabbit; his father was never like this. He ran to the stairs, crying.

"But Matthew, we haven't had the Bible reading yet," Lydia pleaded.

"Lydia, why do you have to undermine my authority at every turn?" Lydia was shocked; he had never shouted at her before. Elsie bolted out of the rocking chair and disappeared upstairs.

Matthew jumped up, grabbed his coat from the hook and stormed out of the house, slamming the door behind him.

Lydia sat, head in hands, weeping. Christian family life wasn't supposed to be like this.

The floorboards creaked, reminding Lydia of the two scared children upstairs. They needed her. Drying her eyes, she fetched the lamp and Bible and went up to them.

"Snuggle into bed now, my dears," she said as calmly as possible. "We will read up here tonight."

She read a Psalm and then prayed.

"…And please, Lord God, help us to live together as a Christian family should. Please forgive us when we don't."

"What about Father?" asked Elsie.

"Where is he?" echoed Charlie.

"I think he just needed some time alone and fresh air," Lydia answered brightly.

"He was in a really foul mood," Charlie observed.

Lydia tucked him in tightly and kissed him on the forehead. "You shouldn't be rude about your father. We all have our off days. And it was wrong of you to kick the ark."

"I didn't mean to."

"Ma, I am so hungry," wined Elsie.

Lydia paused. What would Matthew think if he found her giving the children milk and biscuits in bed, especially as Charlie had been sent up there? But she hated the thought of them going to sleep hungry. She wanted to be a united front with Matthew, but not an unreasonable front. She felt he had more to apologise about than they had. If he had been her son, such a silly, petulant display of anger would have been punished.

"Now, not a word about this, but I will creep down and fetch you your milk and biscuits. Father wouldn't want you to go to bed hungry, would he?" She put her finger to her lips, and the children grinned.

That night, Lydia lay facing the wall. When Matthew eventually came to bed, she feigned sleep but remained awake far longer than him.

CHAPTER 14

The minister's wife, Mrs Relf, listened intently as Suzie poured out her rather incoherent story.

"Well, my dear, you have had a difficult time." She put her hand on Suzie's shoulder. "But I don't think there is much that a good warm bath, a hot meal, and a comfortable bed won't mend." She was secretly relieved that the tale of woe was no worse.

Such kindness and ideas of comfort broke Suzie's fragile composure, and she burst into tears. Everything was going to be all right.

In a haze of hunger, tiredness, and relief, Suzie found herself being taken to the manse and treated like a princess. Mrs Relf and her equally compassionate and capable housemaid soon lit a fire in the spare room and prepared a warm bath and a hot brick in the bed. Suzie felt terribly guilty,

"But what about the minister's dinner?" she blurted out, having fretted over the question since entering the house.

"Mr Relf has probably finished eating and is already snoozing in front of the fire, my dear." His wife reassured her with a smile. "Martha here pops home during the last hymn to ensure the food is ready when he comes in. Preaching gives him a ferocious appetite."

"But what about you? I am messing up your day."

"What nonsense, child!" exclaimed Mrs Relf. "What is the point of our faith if we can't show a little hospitality when we need to? Now, you get into this bath while it is still warm. Martha has left you a nighty just there, and when you are tucked up in bed, I will bring you a nice bowl of soup."

Relaxing in bed, dressed in a voluminous nighty, and sipping delicious soup, Suzie felt overwhelmed with gratitude. Her thousands of cries of "Lord, help me!" had been heard after all. She put the empty soup bowl on the bedside table and sank back into the soft-feather pillows. She pulled the crisp, starched sheet up to her chin and felt the comforting weight of the eiderdown on her weary limbs. Rain lashed against the bedroom window, but she was warm, dry, and safe. She had never been in such a lovely little bedroom. The wallpaper was white, with beautiful blue flowers on delicate green branches curling up to the picture rail. The floorboards were painted white, and so was the wooden furniture. A blue and green rag rug lay by the bed. It was all so perfectly practical and pretty. Before she knew it, Suzie fell into a deep and dreamless sleep.

The sun had already set by the time Suzie awoke. Instead of feeling refreshed, she felt dull in the head, and her throat was sore. She didn't want to make a fuss and put her kind hostess into any more trouble. Being ill away from home was embarrassing. Not knowing what to do, Suzie snuggled deeper under the covers and did nothing. Eventually, Martha crept in to draw the curtains.

"Martha," croaked a small voice from under the blankets, "I'm really sorry, but I think I have caught a cold."

Having felt Suzie's brow for heat, the housemaid nodded. "Wearing wet clothes is a sure way of catching a chill. The damp gets right into the bones. I hope it hasn't gone to your chest. I'll get you a mustard poultice to help prevent it from settling there. And you need a woollen vest to regulate your temperature. And you must not sit in the draught line between the window and the chimney."

Suzie was impressed by her knowledge of medical science. All she could do in her weakness was to lie back and meekly accept Martha's administration.

By Tuesday, despite or because of Martha's medicines, Suzie was beginning to feel better. A telegram had been sent to her parents, and arrangements were being made for her collection. Suzie's clothes were returned, washed, ironed, and well-aired. Any awkwardness she felt about going downstairs and intruding into the Relfs' home life soon evaporated. Mr Relf was as welcoming as his wife. Suzie thought he must be the loveliest grandfather ever. He had a kind, friendly face and a twinkle in his eye. He told amusing stories about his mischievous boyhood, gently teased his wife, showed great interest in Suzie's life, and prayed as if he were really talking to his father.

Tuesday evening found the threesome sitting around the front room fire. Mrs Relf was knitting, and the others were reading books. After a while, Mr Relf put down his book and stretched his legs.

"Suzanne, would you crack me some nuts from the bowl, please?" Suzie was pleased to stop her pretence of reading and do something useful.

"So, what are you going to do when you get home?" he asked.

"I need to find another job as soon as possible," replied Suzie. "Our farm isn't much more than a small hold. It would never make us rich at the best of times, but at the moment, I don't think it is doing more than just paying the rent."

"It must be tough for your parents to work so hard with so little to show for it," he sympathised.

"And they need to pay for John's apprenticeship—they want him to have better prospects than they ever did."

"So, you need to help fund that?"

"Yes, my pay helps."

Suzie paused. Was it really fair that she had to work hard to pay for him to prosper? She had hardly given it thought before. It was just a given fact—boys had to have opportunities. They will hopefully be husbands and fathers someday and need to be breadwinners. Hopefully, somewhere, the family of her future husband was making sacrifices for him to prosper, for her good. That is life. *Her future husband;* the vague thought of the anonymous man gave her a warm feeling in her heart. She handed more walnuts to Mr Relf.

"Your parents must be thankful for having a good daughter," he observed.

Suzie grunted. W*as she a good daughter?*

"Are they both believers?" he asked, holding out his hand for more.

"Oh yes!" Suzie assured him. "It is very important to them."

"And what about you?"

Suzie looked away; she had never been asked such a direct question about her soul in all her life. How could she reply?

Playing with the nutcrackers, she hesitantly started, "I don't know. I want to be, but I don't know if God wants me." She rolled a walnut between her fingers and continued, "I know God can save me, but I don't know if He is willing to." Now that she had started, she may as well continue, however awful it sounded, "I seem to be more willing than He is, but I know that can't be true. I think I have got it all wrong! I sometimes think I will be the only one on judgement day who will say, "I tried to come, but it didn't work." Just voicing the words was awful, especially in a preacher's home. It was like criticising meat while staying with a butcher.

Her tearful eyes looked into Mr Relf's, and she saw sympathy.

"Suzanne, what would make you believe the promise was for you? Think of John 3 verse 16:

'For God so loved the world, that he gave his only begotten Son, that whosoever believeth in him should not perish, but have everlasting life'.

"Imagine it read, 'For God so loved Suzanne Griffen, that He gave, etc.' Would you believe then?"

Suzie thought, "I am not sure. It might be another Suzanne Griffen, not me."

"Exactly, my dear, that is why it says 'Whosoever.'"

Suzie liked that word—whosoever. But there was another problem. "What if I think I am believing, but it isn't really?"

"Do you remember what the Lord Jesus had to say about the size of faith? He said that even small faith, the size of a tiny grain of mustard seed, is powerful. It isn't the size of our faith; it is who we put our faith in that counts. And besides that, in the gospels, we have a lovely prayer to copy: 'I believe, help thou my unbelief.'"

"But what if I come and He doesn't want me?"

"Who makes you want to come to Jesus, Suzanne? Don't keep looking at your emotions and feelings; look into the Bible. Jesus says, 'No man cometh unto me except the Father in heaven draw him.' He is the one who starts the process, and what He begins, He always completes."

Mr Relf finished another nut.

"Look at all the wonderful promises in the Bible. God didn't put them in there to bind Himself into saving us because His love might wane or become disillusioned with humans after a while. His love is so great that He willingly does that without any legal contract being necessary. But He made the promises for our sakes, so we can trust Him and really understand He means what He says and will never change."

"Think of a man and woman on their wedding day. They say wedding vows. On the day, they almost seem irrelevant. They are so in love, they can't imagine ever having a tiff or feeling out of love. But the years go by, and they have a few arguments and some very cold days. Those are the times they have to think of their vows and keep going. Jesus isn't like that. His love is no colder today than when he voluntarily went to the cross for sinners. His invitations are still as warm and sincere."

Here, Mrs Relf chimed in,

"The important thing is to take Jesus at His word. He is totally trustworthy. What He says, you have to believe. The devil wants us to listen to our emotions and feelings. He wants us to sit about, waiting for some amazing bolt from heaven or Damascus experience that will answer all our doubts. He doesn't mind if we sit waiting all our lives until we end up in hell—having never taken Jesus at His word."

Suzie stared into the fire. They had given her so much to think about.

"I should be able to trust the God who helped me so kindly during these last few days."

"Yes," agreed Mr Relf, "That's what the verse: 'Taste and see that the Lord is good' means. We experience His goodness in some situations, which helps us trust Him for the future, even our eternal future."

CHAPTER 15

Lydia felt her shoulders tense as she heard a knock on her front door. She had been expecting the call all morning. Discarding her apron and adjusting a wayward hairpin, she hurried to answer.

"Good morning, Mrs Griffen, I assume?" A smartly dressed, self-assured-looking lady greeted Lydia, who immediately felt shabby.

"You are correct, and you must be Mrs Thompson?" She forced herself to smile and say, "Please, do come in."

Mrs Thompson nodded. "I won't, if you don't mind. I would rather get straight on with the business."

"Very well. I lit the stove, so there should be a bit of warmth in the cottage. I'll find you the key."

When Mr Baillie became ill, Matthew and Lydia suggested that his only daughter should be informed. The proposal was met with a vigorous shaking of the head. "Gwendoline's far too busy to be troubled by me," he wheezed. "She's a good girl and writes when she can." Lydia couldn't understand how a good daughter could be so neglectful of her aged father. After his death, Lydia hunted through his piles of letters, but although the daughter wrote regularly, none of them contained her full address. By the time Lord D'Egerton's estate manager had written to Mr Baillie's cousin (who in the distant past had been his guarantor), and the said cousin had written to Gwendoline, her father had already been committed to the dust. Now, the estate manager was agitating for the cottage and small holdings to be cleared and made ready for new tenants.

Lydia led the way to the house via the unofficial short cut through the vegetable patch and paddock they had created to make life easier. Soon, that would have to be blocked off again. Glancing back at her companion's shiny boots and lace-trimmed skirt, she regretted her decision.

"Sorry, I forgot how soggy it can be along here."

Mrs Thompson continued her dainty steps in silence.

"The lock can be awfully stiff."

No response.

Once inside the cottage, Lydia stoked the stove and surveyed the cluttered kitchen. No one would believe how much tidying she and Matthew had done already, and there was still so much to do—*how would this neat and prim lady clear the house single-handed?* Mrs Thompson quickly set her carpet bag on the table and pulled out an apron. Losing no time at all, she filled the kettle and several saucepans with water, put them on the stove to heat, and located a bucket under the sink. Lydia was about to wish her well and head for the door when she caught a glimpse of her face and saw eyes brimming with tears.

"Would you like me to stay and help?" The words popped out before Lydia had even thought about them.

"You don't have to."

"No, but I am offering to. There is much work to be done, and two is better than one." Lydia sounded as if she were reasoning with an upset child. "I can just run across and get my apron, cleaning equipment, and some tea, then we can make a plan of action. Can't we?"

The only reply she received was a weak smile and a tiny nod.

The first half an hour of working together was terribly awkward. Mrs Thompson remained forbiddingly silent. *Does she disapprove of what I have done? Did I overstep the mark by rearranging the house to make it easier for her father? Should we really have started clearing and burning old things without her permission?* Pondering things from an outsider's perspective, Lydia felt very uneasy. Without conferring, Mrs Thompson packed belongings into boxes, and Lydia scrubbed the walls. They politely worked around each other. The long silence filled the room, making it claustrophobic.

"You must wonder why I have been such a neglectful daughter." Lydia jumped in shock at this sudden thunderbolt. She continued to studiously scrub the wall.

"Umm, well, now."

"Of course you do. You have been here, kindly caring for him while his one and only daughter has been conspicuous by her absence."

"I was pleased to help. We were very fond of your father. He had been a good neighbour for many years."

"But I should have been here. I so wish I had been." The words erupted as a sob.

Lydia dropped her scrubbing brush and rushed over to the steaming kettle.

"Let's sit down and have a nice cup of tea." She busied herself with drink preparations while her companion regained her composure. *Sitting and drinking tea together will be even more awkward than working.* Gwendoline cleared two chairs and the end of the kitchen table. Sitting opposite each other, the ladies stared deep into their teacups as if they had never seen the beverage before.

Once again, it was Gwendoline who broke the silence.

"Four years ago, I was widowed. All three of my daughters were still at home. Our small savings rapidly dwindled. I am a seamstress—" Lydia looked up with interest. They both sipped their tea.

"For the last three years, I have worked long hours, building up a small dress-making business from our front room. My older two daughters are now married, but the youngest, Jane, still lives at home and works with me."

"You have had a difficult time," sympathised Lydia.

"This winter, Jane caught scarlet fever. For weeks, I nursed her. Her life hung in the balance for many weeks. She recovered but was left blind."

"Oh, how terribly sad!"

"Even if I had known about dear Father, I couldn't have come."

"I am pleased you were unaware. At least you didn't have that dilemma to deal with—God knows when it is best to keep us from knowing things."

"Indeed, He kindly does!" agreed Gwendoline with such hearty conviction that Lydia immediately recognised she was in the company of a fellow pilgrim. The tension in the room instantly lifted.

"And how is poor Jane?" asked Lydia.

"She is still blind, but thankfully, her reasoning and brain power are not affected as we feared they might be. She is slowly learning to cope and even managing to sew a simple seam."

Lydia poured more tea.

"I have had to employ a local girl to help with the dress business. She is coming on nicely."

"And where is Jane while you are here?"

"She is staying with my firstborn, Marion, for the week. A change of routine is good for her."

Once again, they sipped in silence, but this time, it felt companionable.

"Did your father know of your straightened means?" asked Lydia, "I never heard him mention your woes."

"No, no. I never mentioned it to him. Maybe I was too proud. Maybe I didn't want to bother him. He had had his fair share of struggles already. Anyway, once I started my little business, I actually started to enjoy it. I have always liked working with fabrics."

"So have I," agreed Lydia, smiling. "Before I married, I was a seamstress for years. I've lost count of how many wedding dresses I've made."

"Do you sew much now?"

"Not a lot. I don't get much time, and my eyesight isn't what it used to be."

It was Gwendoline's turn to look sympathetic. "You probably need a pair of reading glasses."

"Or a few more hours in a day," smiled Lydia. "So many things demand a woman's attention, don't they?"

"Quite," agreed Gwendoline, staring out the window. "But would we really want it any other way? Imagine being surrounded by servants in a large manor. How would you fill your day?"

"With piano practice and making personalised greeting cards?"

"Flower arranging and horse riding?"

"Or maybe just sitting about drinking tea with congenial company for far too long?" laughed Lydia, standing up to get back to work.

"Using one's best Wedgewood tea set," continued Gwendoline in a posh falsetto voice, waving her father's sturdy clay cup.

At the end of the week, Lydia walked her new friend to the stagecoach and waved until it had disappeared around the corner. With mingled sadness and thankfulness, she wandered back home. What a joy it was to unexpectedly discover a new friend! A person with whom one could giggle like a girl or have a deep heart-to-heart conversation. Together, they had emptied and cleared the cottage, fed a roaring bonfire, sold unwanted items on a stall at the garden gate, and transferred fruit bushes to the Griffen's Garden—all with gusto and good humour. Gwen had slept at her father's cottage but had joined the family for her meals. Matthew had risen out of his gloom to help with the projects when extra muscle power was required. His table conversation also had sparks of positivity. Elsie was delighted to have someone to show her how to do a smocking stitch, and Charlie enjoyed manning the stall after school. To crown it all, Gwen had found a pair of reading glasses in the back of a draw. At her insistence, Lydia tried them on and found them surprisingly helpful. The children chuckled at the sight of her extra-big eyes in the heavy frames, but Lydia just laughed back with delight. Hopefully, this was the end of blurred words and stitches, squinting, and headaches.

CHAPTER 16

Suzie's father arranged for her to return home on a cabbage cart. To be more precise, a cart load of cabbages from Brookfield had been sent up to Covent Garden Market, and she caught a lift on the tranter's return journey. What she hadn't bargained for was the elongated route home, thanks to the tranter's entrepreneurial spirit. When the cabbages went, the sugar beet came. Every inch of the cart was full of them—fresh from and accompanied by the dark soil of East Anglia. Suzie jogged and jigged up and down on the hard wooden bench as they wended their way through the countryside along pot-holed lanes and rough farm tracks, selling the beet to farmers for animal fodder. Every farmer wrangled at the price, and a lengthy bargaining ritual was painstakingly played out. Suzie learnt the irritating sales pitch word for word. The grower was "a top-class producer." The sugar beets were the "best I've had the pleasure to see this year," and the price was "under-cutting any other seller." In short, this was a "one-off opportunity; take it or leave it." Suzie slumped with disappointment every time a farmer decided to leave it and hoped that someone would soon take it all and be done with it. Finally, as dusk was falling, a tired, stiff, and hungry Suzie descended from the cart at Brookfield village and tottered her way home.

It felt wonderful to be back in the warm embrace of her family. Ma plied her with soup and sympathy, and Pa kindly cleaned her muddy boots. Elsie showed her a beautifully smocked dress she was working on, and Charlie wanted to hear the details of her dismissal over and over again, enjoying the horror of the injustice. Brandishing a wooden sword, he breathed out threats and slaughter on Mr Briggs until Pa angrily snatched it out of his hand and threw it across the room with more than necessary force. The sword broke, and Charlie ran upstairs, crying. Suzie was shocked and perturbed at feeling a thorn in the family nest.

A few days after Suzie's return home, the first lamb of the season was born. All the family came to admire the new-born as he attempted a wobbly lunge towards his mother's swollen udder. Soon, there was no time to discuss Lydia's future, as every waking hour was filled with delivering lambs, bottle-feeding, and sheep husbandry. Clad in an old frock bespattered with milk and mud and her windswept hair decorated with strands of hay, Suzie was in her element. Her small hands and strong arms were just the right combination for helping with difficult deliveries. The spring sun quickly thawed the night frosts and gave an energising warmth. The trees budded, and the birds and all creation sang of renewal and hope, except Mr Griffen. Working so closely with her father was normally one of the delights of lambing for Suzie, but this year, he seemed out of sorts. He moaned and groaned. He huffed and puffed. The ewes were stupid. Their milk was too thick or too watery. The lambs were senseless. The man who had taught Suzie to be calm and patient around the sheep was irritable and impatient. She wanted to ask him what was wrong but did not dare.

"Whatever is wrong with Pa?" She asked her mother.

Lydia glanced around the kitchen anxiously.

"I expect he is just tired today," she replied in a hushed tone.

"Today? He's been like that all week!" remonstrated Suzie.

"Hush, child!" begged her mother. "Lambing is a busy time."

"As if I don't know that!"

Suzie suddenly felt awful for attacking her mother. "I'm sorry, but he manages without being so grumpy most lambing seasons."

"He has had a tough year."

"But that doesn't mean he can forget his pleases, thank yous, and common courtesies."

"Be patient with him, Suzie," pleaded Lydia.

"Be patient with who?" demanded Matthew, barging through the back door.

Lydia and Suzie looked like they had been caught with their fingers in the honey.

"We all have to be patient with one another, don't we, dear? Especially this busy time of year," answered his wife soothingly.

"Humph! And when exactly is a quiet time of the year in farming?" snarled Matthew.

Suzie saw pain in her mother's eyes and scurried unhappily off to the lambing pens. The sun was hidden behind a large grey cloud, and the birds no longer sang.

There was some truth in Matthew's sour comment about never having a quiet time in the farming year, and as the weeks rolled on, Suzie still found plenty to do. As much as her father needed her on the farm, she knew a wage was even more needed. Previously, she had relied on Pa to find her a job, but now, she felt she would only be adding to his burdens, so she started to enquire herself. Most jobs in Brookfield were somehow linked to the D'Egerton family or estate. Suzie vowed she would never work for them again, and anyway, probably in their eyes, she had blotted her copybook and was unemployable.

Eventually, it was the pastor's wife who came up with the perfect solution. One of the deacons, Mr Mortimer, had become a widower the previous year. His mother had stayed several months to help care for his two young daughters but had now returned home. A live-in maid cum nanny was required to attend to the day-to-day running of the house. Suzie was aghast at the suggestion that she could manage the task. Running a house and being a substitute mother sounded far too involved and grown-up.

"But there is not one aspect of household management you have not been involved in, Suzie," argued her mother. "You have always helped me with the younger ones. You have cooked meals, and think of all the new skills you learnt at the big house."

All arguments were swept away when Suzie attended an interview. Mr Mortimer seemed like a sombre but sensible man. His daughters were chubby and sweet, his house was elegant but comfortable, and the salary was decidedly generous. Suzie's youth and inexperience did not seem to be an issue. Before leaving the house, she had signed up to begin first thing the following Monday morning.

Arriving promptly at seven o'clock the following week, Suzie was even more delighted to be ushered in by a maid. *I have someone under me!* The stove and fire had already been lit. Once Suzie had unpacked in her spacious attic room and changed into a rather becoming black housemaid's dress, it was time to wake the girls. Prudence and Constance were aged six and four. They seemed delighted with the novelty of a new person waking them up, and they chattered away happily. They could dress independently but wanted to show Suzie everything in their bedroom and wardrobe. Suzie looked anxiously at the hall clock—it would not do for them to run late on her first morning. There were two dining rooms downstairs. One was to be used only on formal occasions or when their father dined with the girls. The smaller and cosier dining room was adjacent to the kitchen. It was here that Suzie would take meals with the girls. Mr Mortimer breakfasted alone in his study.

Maggie, the undermaid, cooked the porridge. All Suzie had to do was give thanks, serve breakfast to the girls, take a tray of food to their father, and then eat her own porridge. *So far, this is less work than being at home!* Prue and Connie wanted to know all about Suzie, her family, and the animals on the farm. After breakfast, Suzie read a chapter from the Children's Story Bible, and then they trotted upstairs to get ready to leave for school. Although the Mortimers lived on the outskirts of Milton, the girls did not attend Milton School. Mr Mortimer preferred his daughters to be educated privately by a lady of the town who had previously taught his sisters. The girls' eyes lit up when Suzie explained that she had no idea where the teacher lived—having to show a grownup the way made them feel very important. Suzie was a bit disappointed when she met the teacher, Mrs Dillerstone. She was a tired, large, and wheezy lady who seemed to have outlived her sense of humour. Her lessons were sure to be dull and dreary. With a mixed sense of sadness at leaving the girls in such a barren environment and relief that she wasn't school-age any longer, Suzie turned and briskly walked back to the Mortimer establishment.

A pattern was soon established. After taking the girls to Mrs Dillerstone, Suzie would return and have coffee with Maggie. She would then divide up the work. Maggie would prepare vegetables, make beds, tend the fires, sweep, scrub floors, and run errands. Suzie would cook, bake, shop, and dust. They shared the Monday laundry duties, much to Maggie's relief, for the grandmother had never involved herself in such things. Maggie came at 7 o'clock and left mid-afternoon. She was older than Suzie but seemed to lack ambition and was content to be told what to do. Suzie found that she required precise instruction; otherwise, she became flustered. Maggie was not a sparkling conversationalist and seemed to have no interests. She lived with her mother somewhere in the back streets of Milton. If it were not for the previous day's newspaper from Mr Mortimer's study, coffee and lunch breaks would have been extremely dull affairs. Sometimes, Suzie read out exciting extracts to Maggie, whose standard replies were, *"Well, I declare!"* but she had nothing to declare, or *"Well, I never did!"* which Suzie could well believe.

Mr Mortimer rarely interfered in the running of the household or his daughters' upbringing. When he wasn't working long hours in an office somewhere in Milford, he hibernated away in his study. Some evenings, he rang the bell and requested the girls' company. Dutifully but not eagerly, Prue and Connie stopped their play and trailed into the study. As quickly as possible, they escaped and re-joined Suzie in the little dining room for games, crafts, or singsongs before bedtime. Suzie's heart was full of love and sympathy for the dear, motherless girls. There was little joy in their lives with Mrs Dreary Dillerstone and Mr Morose Mortimer. Despite feeling tired by the end of the day, Suzie tried to be as lively and fun as possible in the evenings. She rummaged through the cupboards and dug out board games to play. They baked biscuits, had dollies' tea parties in a den under the dining room table, and made paper chain people. Every night, when they were tucked up in bed, she told them made-up stories about the adventures their dolls got up to while they were at Mrs Dillerstone's. The stories that made them most giggle and plead for more were tales about the dolls being naughty, flying through Mrs Dillerstone's kitchen window and secretly causing all sorts of mischief.

As the evenings grew longer and the weather warmer, Suzie took Prue and Connie for walks. Never before in their lives had they been allowed to stomp through puddles, jump over streams, or climb trees. As long as they were clean and tidy before their appearance in the study, their father would be none the wiser, and it was guaranteed he would never ask. On rare occasions, when Suzie knew Mr Mortimer would be late home or not require dinner, she walked the girls down to her parents' house. There, Elsie took them under her wing and showed them all the animals. Charlie showed off to them and was rewarded by gasps of horrified admiration. Lydia always eked the meal to feed her little guests. Matthew sometimes walked halfway back with Suzie, carrying a tired Connie on his shoulders. Prue thought the Griffen's house was 'the best in the whole wide world'. That made Suzie feel both happy and sad.

Every Thursday, Mr Mortimer's sister visited for the day and took over the reins to give Suzie the day off. Suzie found it hard to believe she had any Mortimer blood flowing through her; she was so different from her brother. Bringing her toddler son with her, Mrs Marianne White sailed into the house at breakfast time, swept the girls into a hearty embrace, and radiated warmth and joy. As Suzie collected her belongings and made her escape, she heard laughter and chatter flowing from the dining room. Even Mr Mortimer glided silently from the depths of his study to greet his vivacious sister.

Ma had assured Suzie that her one precious day off a week was her own and she should not feel obliged to come home and work, but Suzie usually found herself gravitating towards home and the animals. As much as she enjoyed the domestic comforts of the Mortimers, she itched to get stuck into an occasional agricultural project. Without even realising it, Suzie was slightly lonely. Her former school friends were busily employed, and one or two were even married. Work at the big house had been tough, but others were always around to observe or talk to. Her parents worked so relentlessly hard that a great sense of loyalty sent her back to help where she could. One Thursday morning, she decided to play the townie and go out for coffee before returning home. Sitting in an elegant tea room and being served a tiny cup of coffee by a snooty waitress and then presented with a huge bill convinced her that a mid-morning drink with her parents was much more her cup of tea.

CHAPTER 17

Caleb wandered around his new cottage with ever-increasing satisfaction. It was just the ticket. There was a front room to the left of the front door and a dining room to the right. Behind it was a good-sized kitchen. Underneath was a large cellar, and above were three bedrooms. The bulky furniture of the previous tenant had been left in place, which was a welcome bonus. His mother's parting gifts of jam, honey, and preserves sat proudly on the shelves of the otherwise empty cellar. But the tablecloth she had sent remained packed. Caleb didn't really see the point of tablecloths—they were only another thing to wash. He was a bachelor and meant to live like one. He would wear his boots into the kitchen. He'd only shave once a week—for church. He would only wash up when he had run out of clean crockery, and his dog, Tish, would be welcome indoors.

He liked what he saw outside, too. No mountain ranges hemmed him in, only gently rolling hills in the distance. The landscape was not harsh and rugged, but mild and tamed. Scotland was still in spring, but Kent was in summer already. It was a terrible time in the farming calendar to take on a farm. It was definitely too late to sow spring barley, and sowing wheat in June was madness, but he would try a couple of acres. Grass in the meadows had grown long through lack of grazing, so he was determined to cut it for hay. There was so much to do and buy, but Caleb was raring to go. But for now, after his long journey south and the less-than-welcoming meeting with the estate manager, all he wanted was a nice cup of tea and a bite to eat. To boil water, he needed to light the stove, and to achieve this, he needed to find firewood. He plodded outside again and looked in the outhouses. One was a woodshed, and thankfully, it still had a pile of seasoned logs. That would be another job—sourcing and seasoning wood. The cold chimney made the fire slow to catch. A warm drink seemed less and less likely. At least, the drinking water tasted reasonable—not nearly as good as Highland water, of course, but passable. Cold water and pickled boiled eggs on an old crust would suffice.

Tish, who had been snoozing happily on a mat by the stove, suddenly pricked up her ears and growled. Caleb looked out the window and saw a female heading towards the kitchen door with a basket. He opened it before she knocked.

"Good afternoon!"

The woman smiled at him and extended her hand, which he duly shook.

"Hello, I am your neighbour, Lydia Griffen. We live just over there." She pointed beyond the orchard and hedge to a cottage identical to his.

Caleb stepped aside and motioned for her to come in. Mrs Griffen stepped straight in and put the basket on the kitchen table. From the basket, she pulled out a pot wrapped in a tea towel. Unwrapping it, she placed the pot on the stove.

"Welcome to Brookfield. I thought you might like a bit of stew. Getting organised can be difficult the first afternoon in a new place, and I expect your chimney is cold."

Caleb was delighted; what a kind and sensible woman! Mrs Griffen looked about the same age as some of his older sisters-in-law. She had the same middle-aged wrinkles—whether they were laughter or careworn lines, they were strangely becoming. Her eyes radiated warmth. Caleb knew instantly that he liked her.

"Thank you, Mrs Griffen; that is so kind. I am Caleb Baker, and this is Tish." His dog seemed to have come to the same conclusion about their visitor and wagged her tail enthusiastically. Lydia gave Tish a quick stroke.

"I understand you are one of John Baker's sons. My husband knew him fairly well."

"News travels," observed Caleb wryly.

"A change of tenant on the estate is big news in these backwaters," smiled Lydia.

Caleb shuddered. Would the locals chew over his every move, success, or failure?

"Don't worry," assured Lydia, as if she could read his mind. "The gossips are in the minority around here. I am sure you will find that most people are supportive and helpful. What farmer isn't generous with his free advice?"

Caleb laughed.

"I'll need all I can get of that, to be sure."

"I'll leave you to settle in, but won't you come across tomorrow? We may be able to lend you a few things."

Back up in Scotland, jokes were often made about the cold, stand-offish nature of Southerners. But, besides their oddly clipped accent and strange vowel pronunciation, Caleb rather liked what he found. By the end of his first week in Kent, Caleb was thoroughly convinced that the Griffens were ideal neighbours. Matthew wasn't exactly the jolliest of men, but he was experienced and generous. He had offered Caleb the use of his horse and plough, and without them, he would never have gotten so far on with the wheat sowing. Now, he didn't have to waste precious time looking around markets for his own plough—that could now wait until after haymaking. Matthew also had useful contacts. He knew a man with a good-milking cow for sale and the best farmer to buy ewe lambs from.

Lydia was thoughtful and motherly. Caleb hadn't come south to be mothered, but it was reassuring to know that he would know who to turn to if he ever felt the need. She claimed to have more broody hens than she knew what to do with and gave one, with all its eggs, to Caleb. He was delighted with his potential flock and found a cosy corner in a fox-proof shed for the viciously protective mother-to-be.

Caleb had already had two delicious meals with the Griffens and a cosy evening at their fireside. It was a privilege to be at their family Bible reading and prayer time. From what he understood, the Griffens were not a very gregarious family, so being welcomed readily into their cottage was an honour. It seemed they had also been very kind to old Mr Baillie, the previous tenant. They hadn't gotten around to closing up the gap in the fence between the two properties and apologised. After a discussion with Caleb, they unanimously agreed to leave it open. Caleb was quickly on teasing and wrestling terms with Charlie. Coming from such a large family of boys, Caleb knew all the moves for playfighting. Charlie was impressed with the speed at which Caleb could get him floored, and even more impressed that he was willing to teach his tricks step by step and get floored himself. Caleb had won a fan, who readily came over to chop wood, clear nettles, and help repair fences. Elsie seemed like a pretty, sweet young girl who would probably turn out to be as caring as her mother. Apparently, there were also two older children working away from home.

One of the most daunting things Caleb did during that first week was to walk into Brookfield's chapel on Sunday. He couldn't take Tish for moral support. He resisted the urge to tag along with the Griffen family. Meeting so many new people would be hard, but soon, he reassured himself, he would just be part of the furniture. He wanted to sneak into the back row, but a deacon in the lobby ushered him halfway down the aisle to a vacant pew. An old man soon joined him, grunted a greeting, and then fidgeted around until he seemed satisfied with his position. Ahead of him, one or two wriggling children stared impertinently at him. Some nudged their older siblings or parents, who were either dignified enough to ignore it or curious enough to glance his way. A few young ladies simpered and blushed when they met his eye. He felt an instant distrust of coquettish girls. Caleb opened his hymnbook to avoid that silly business and studiously read until the service commenced. Having grown up in Scotland, Caleb had only sung psalms in kirk. Many Scottish believers would have refused to even mime a man-made hymn during worship. Caleb had already decided what to do before he left his parents' house—unless the hymn contents were erroneous, he would sing with all good conscience. A brief perusal of the hymnal gave him no reason for concern. Many of the hymns were ones they had sung at home on Sabbath evenings during winter months.

During the service, Caleb marvelled at the wonderfully transcendent truth of the Bible that was beyond time and space. Here in rural Kent, he listened to the Word of God, just as his family were hundreds of miles away. And here, in this chapel, over thirty-five years ago, the Lord had met with his dad and converted him. The minister preached warmly and well from Joshua 1 v 5, *"As I was with Moses, so I will be with thee: I will not fail thee, nor forsake thee."* Caleb felt full of thankfulness to the Lord for His love and trustworthiness.

After the service, the old man who had sat in the same pew as Caleb turned to him and struck up a conversation, or rather, a monologue. As the building slowly emptied, Caleb was given a thorough briefing on all the man's aches and pains. Caleb's sympathetic noises seemed to encourage the man to expound further on their causes and respective treatments. He could predict the weather with his right knee, and only goose fat from male birds was good for preventing pneumonia. Caleb rightly guessed that the man rarely had a new and captive audience, so he was determined to make the most of the opportunity. But he decided enough was enough when the old gent moved on from joints to his digestive system. Caleb stood up, put his hand on the man's shoulder, and said, "You're a brave soldier, but I mustn't keep you." With that, the sufferer, content with the sympathy, let Caleb pass and cordially bade him a good day, leaving Caleb asking himself why he hadn't tried that manoeuvre sooner. Yet, the lengthy medical consultation worked to Caleb's advantage. By the time he had left the chapel, the congregation had dispersed, making it possible for him to travel home without having to engage in social pleasantries.

CHAPTER 18

The summer was as good as the previous one, which was bad. The sun and rain came in good measure, swelling the grain, apples, and pears. The grass was lush, and the lambs fattened in record time. Suzie was glad that the atmosphere at home had improved somewhat. Her mother had been able to take up sewing again, thanks to Mr Baillie's old glasses. She and Elsie were beginning to be in demand locally for clothing repairs and alterations. The addition to the family income was welcome. Suzie's father seemed re-energised by their new neighbour. Suzie had only exchanged a few words with Caleb Baker, but from all she had heard from her parents, he seemed to be a pleasant chap. He and her father worked together on various farm projects, helping each other, lending equipment, and exchanging ideas. The friendly support he offered Suzie's father contrasted sharply and painfully with her brother John's behaviour. Every now and again, she felt resentment build up within her against John; so much money went directly from her wages and the measly farm profits to fund his apprenticeship. She wondered if he had any idea what a heavy yoke the indenture had placed on his poor parents' stooping shoulders—not to mention her own. At the very least, they deserved regular, chatty letters from him, but he only wrote if he needed anything. She had never, ever received a letter from him. Sometimes, she was tempted to write to him, setting out exactly how much she was funding him each month, but she thought it would probably be a waste of a postal stamp. This was the way of the world: women make sacrifices for men. She understood that and was willingly prepared to do so for her father and a husband, but for a brother? Suzie tried to smother her resentment as soon as it raised its ugly head, and she asked the Lord to remove it. Bitter thoughts could eat away inside like cancer and harm her soul.

Talking of brothers, Charlie had fallen under the spell of the new neighbour and had spent all the summer holiday helping on the farm. Suzie was delighted to hear that he was so useful and willing to learn. She hoped Pa and Charlie would grow in their appreciation of each other. Her only regret was that she didn't have more time during the summer to help at home.

At the beginning of the summer, she was informed that she would have two weeks off while the girls were on a beach holiday with their father, Mr and Mrs White and their little cousin. She skipped home like a schoolgirl to tell her parents. A whole fortnight working in sunbathed fields alongside her Pa and wearing scruffy clothes! Feeling a warm breeze on her face and ruffling her hair, the thought was delightful. Also, drinking the refreshing lemonade Ma always made for harvest workers, and then luxuriating her weary limbs in her own cosy bed at the end of each long day, the whole picture made her want to sing for joy. It would also be quite nice to get to know their new neighbour a bit more.

But, at the very last minute, Mr Mortimer declared he was too busy at work with the ledgers to go on frivolous seaside trips that had been thrust upon him against his will. Without considering the inconvenience, he abruptly instructed Suzie to go instead. Suzie could have cried and stamped her feet with disappointment and impotent rage. Mrs White was furious with her brother, but Prue and Connie danced with delight at the idea of Suzie going with them.

"We'll show you our lovely guest house with the big rocking horse and dolls' house."

"How wonderful!" *But I would have preferred to be wheat-harvesting.*

"We can make huge sandcastles!"

"That will be exciting." *My poor parents!*

"You can paddle in the sea!"

"Lovely, I have always wanted to do that." *Whenever will I get to sleep in my own bed again?*

"We can have sausages and bacon every day for breakfast if we want to."

"Utterly delicious, but now you must let me run upstairs and pack my bag. I also need to write a quick note to my mother and inform her of the change of plan."

With a heart feeling heavier than her luggage, Suzie climbed into the White's empty carriage. Each rotation of the wheels conveyed her further away from her parent's farm and her dream of a small slice of home life. Prue and Connie bounced from one window to the next, chatting excitedly about all they saw. By the time they had reached the White's house, Suzie's head was thumping, and waves of motion sickness washed over her.

"Welcome, my lovely ladies!" called out Mrs White as she embraced her nieces. She glanced beyond them at Suzie. "Oh, you poor girl, you look as white as a sheet! The carriage springs are rather—well, rather overly springy." Suzie staggered out, relieved to be on *terra firma*.

"Prue and Connie, you run along and find little Thomas." Turning towards Suzie, she smiled pityingly. "And what you need is a good lie down. I have made up the spare room bed for you for the night. Go there now, have a good sleep, maybe a good cry, and then you will be as fresh as a daisy for the train ride tomorrow."

Suzie put on a brave smile, thanked her, and did exactly as she was told. As well as a good cry, she let out her frustration by beating the pillows, then had a good long doze. Supper was brought up on a tray—Suzie wasn't sure if that was Mrs White being kind or Mrs White side-stepping the thorny dilemma of where to seat Suzie—with the family or with the servants.

For the entire fortnight, Suzie found herself in this strange no-man's land. Mr and Mrs White went out of their way to make her feel welcome and appreciated, but her opinions and wishes were never sought or enquired after. Even at their warmest, the Whites left Suzie in no doubt that she was not their equal, and they were graciously bestowing kindness. When they were dining alone, she was welcome to sit with the family in the guest house dining room, but when they entertained friends and relatives, no place was set for her.

When with just the family, Mrs White linked arms with Suzie as they followed the skipping children to the beach, joined in the sandcastle building, and enthusiastically engaged in rock-pooling adventures. Other times, without prior notice, she and Mr White just disappeared—to concerts, museums, shops, or who knows where—leaving Suzie with all three children. The responsibility of looking after them all on a crowded beach robbed Suzie much of the pleasure that a day at the seaside normally offers, especially as Thomas was prone to toddle off towards the water's edge, then fly into a screaming tantrum when intercepted. Between the three of them, the children seemed determined to experience every hazard a day at the beach could afford. Thomas dropped his food in the sand and howled at the texture. Prue rubbed her face after making a sand castle and got some grains in her eye, and then Connie stepped on a stinging jellyfish. Thomas again wandered off following a stranger, Prue fell on slippery seaweed when rock pooling and got a black eye, and Connie needed rescuing by a friendly swimmer after being buffeted by pounding waves. And why was it that when they finally settled on the beach, one of them always suddenly needed the water closet ?

But the worst days were when friends and family joined them on the beach. The doting relatives entertained the children, demoting Suzie to the roles of burden bearer, deck chair finder, and ice cream buyer. The moment Suzie sat down and opened a book to read, someone would find a little job that needed doing. Suzie wondered if this was how a spinster aunt would feel—very useful for doing what others would prefer not to do. The best days were when Mr and Mrs White took all the children off to visit others. Suzie was then free to do whatever she pleased.

The guest house proprietress seemed to have a soft spot for Suzie and generously supplied her with sandwiches, sausage rolls, and turnovers for her expeditions. But, oh, how she wished that her parents and younger siblings could enjoy the luxury of a holiday. How much more fun it would be to explore places with them! How wonderful it would be for her mother to have meals prepared for her and laundry returned promptly, all clear, ironed, and aired! Suzie felt annoyed when she overheard her fellow guests complaining over petty matters to the hardworking boarding-house staff—some people don't realise how fortunate they were. Such treats seemed wasted on them. Once or twice, she couldn't stop herself from winking at the poor maids as they stood silently, listening to an undeserved tirade of criticism. Maybe that is why she was given such generously packed lunches.

Suzie had never been to the seaside before and thoroughly enjoyed exploring the coves, walking along the cliff-top path, and browsing the little shops. Having the liberty and time to wander where she pleased was a wonderful novelty. Sometimes, Suzie sat on the harbour wall, munched on her lunch, and people-watched. Along came an elegant young lady, richly dressed in an impractical white dress. She wore a beautiful bonnet and shaded herself with a parasol. Suzie cast her as the beloved daughter of a rich merchant. She had just finished her education in a genteel establishment that prepared young ladies to be docile wives and dotting mothers. From dawn to dusk, she could revel in relaxation and pleasure. Soon, she would be presented at the palace and be available for marriage offers. Right now, she was off to one of the stylish boutiques in the high street for a fitting of a new evening gown. Her father would pick up the bill. Here, Suzie's fantasy turned into questions. Would such a daughter know anything of the freedom Suzie was enjoying today? The staid woman in black, just a few paces behind her, was probably a servant sent to mind her. Would her father, then later, her husband, ever fully trust her to venture alone beyond their front door? Could this beautiful creature marry for love, or would her father orchestrate her matrimony like any other of his advantageous business dealings? Suzie shuddered at the boredom of a life of tedious afternoon teas, piano recitations, and dabbling in watercolours. A few days of relaxation sufficed her.

Looking down towards the water's edge, Suzie saw a group of lasses washing out lobster pots. An angry man remonstrated with a burly brunette girl, swore at her, then staggered off down an alley. The girl totally ignored the incident and busied herself sorting fish. Once the man was out of sight, she muttered something that made the gang of girls roar with laughter. Suzie placed her as a fisherman's daughter. She had been sorting fish, mending nets, and rushing between the harbour and fish stall since infancy, gradually taking over the work from her prematurely aged mother. She knew her worth; she could mend nets faster, sort fish quicker, and sell fish better than any other fisherwoman. A sharp snarl from her father after a mediocre night on choppy waters was to be expected. Beneath the grouching lay mutual reliance and respect. As far back as the family could remember, their men had gone to sea, and their women had worked at the shoreline, anxiously watched weather and waves, and nursed chapped hands. The brunette could expect to marry one of her kind and produce the next generation of seafarers.

Once she was over the disappointment of not being at home and the feeling of guilt at relaxing while her parents were working so hard, Suzie bounced back and enjoyed the time she had to herself. Since her conversation with the Relfs, Suzie had more spiritual peace. Instead of looking at her feelings, she was learning to look at the facts. She grasped God's promises with both hands and rested on His unchangeable character. If He, the Creator and Sustainer of all things, was satisfied with the arrangement of Christ being a substitute for all who trust in Him, then she could be satisfied too. This change of thinking didn't come easily. She still had times of doubt and unbelief, but she was learning to use a relevant scriptural verse to fight them. It was such a comfort to realise that God's magnificent plan of salvation was so sure and firm, His promises so genuine, and His character so trustworthy. She knew she could entrust her life, soul, and eternity to Him, and she did so. It was disappointing not to have some wonderful conversion experience—a spiritual swoon, ecstatic joy, or something else other people sometimes have. All she could do was rest on the promises and character of Jesus and trust Him. She loved the verse, "We love him because he first loved us." It answered many of her misgivings and focused her mind away from her poor, weak, and changeable love to His, which is eternal and powerful to save to the uttermost.

CHAPTER 19

Caleb returned from the morning service and flopped into his armchair. He had just declined an invitation to the Griffens for Sunday dinner and was now regretting it. He was sure he had hurt Lydia's feelings a little, something he had no intention of doing. Whatever possessed him to turn down the offer of an abundant and well-cooked meal? He hadn't bothered lighting his stove, so a hot meal was out of the question. Something had irritated him, and he couldn't be bothered to figure out what it was. Maybe it was the hot weather and insufficient sleep due to the heat. It could be general exhaustion or it could be Mr Mortimer sitting too close to Suzie Griffen this morning. Caleb was displeased with himself for being irked by the situation. It was absolutely none of his business. The Mortimer's pew was directly in front of where he normally sat. Usually, the two little girls sat between the adults. Having Suzie in his direct line of vision was no hardship to Caleb. She looked becoming in her Sunday frock, and unlike the other silly, smirking young ladies, Suzie always looked fully engaged with the service. She sang the alto part melodiously, followed the Bible reading with her finger for one of the little girls, and attentively listened to the sermon, sometimes even nodding her head in agreement.

Today, there had been a bit of a kerfuffle when the Mortimers had walked in. Instead of leading the way, Mr Mortimer pushed his oldest daughter ahead of him. On sitting down, he removed the smaller girl from her place between him and Suzie, sat her briefly on his lap, then shuffled along the pew towards Suzie and plonked the little girl next to her sister. The girls looked put out by the arrangement and whispered their protests, but their father sat ramrod straight and ignored them. Suzie seemed to blush. Caleb thought she edged closer to the end of the pew after the first hymn, but he may have been mistaken.

Caleb was annoyed with himself for caring. He had hardly admitted to himself the disappointment of Suzie not going home to help with the harvest. He hadn't realised that he was looking forward to working with her and getting to know her better. This was not what he had planned. He wanted to be immune to the charms of the opposite sex for at least a few more years. He did not want to be hurt again. Suzie looked sensible and nice, but so had Annella l. Maybe he was just a poor judge of character.

He was also a bit annoyed with Suzie. Was she encouraging that cold and starchy Mortimer? Surely she couldn't find him attractive? Being a prim and proper wife to such a staid and correct man wouldn't suit her at all. He had seen Suzie on her parent's farm—her uninhibited enthusiasm and freeness. Would she surrender all that for that hideous man? If so, she was not the girl he imagined her to be. Could she be just another calculating woman who can put her feelings aside to marry for wealth, ease, and social standing? Is the way to a woman's heart through one's wallet and bank balance? Caleb shuddered.

Looking around his bare and basic kitchen, Caleb suddenly saw his surroundings through the eyes of a young woman. What could he offer any potential partner besides companionship? The poor girl would have to slog as hard as he did for an uncertain and often disappointing income. A pen-pushing towny worked regular hours, never trod mud into the house, earned enough to keep a maid, gave his wife a generous dress allowance for gowns, and…

Tish nuzzled against Caleb's leg and looked up into his eyes enquiringly. Caleb rubbed his muzzle and was rewarded by an enthusiastic tailwag.

"Yes, I know I am being silly, just sitting here moping. Don't worry; there's nothing wrong with me, just a pathetic moment of self-pity. I should be finding a crust for lunch, shouldn't I? You and I rub along well together, don't we?" The dog's brown eyes conveyed deep sympathy and trust. "We like this way of life, even if no one else does." Tish thumped his tail in agreement on the flagstone floor.

Fetching the milk, cheese, and butter out of the cellar, a few slices of gammon from the meat safe, some salad leaves and tomatoes from the kitchen garden, and a loaf and pot of pickle from the cupboard, Caleb cobbled together a substantial cold lunch. Tish looked hopefully at the feast and was rewarded with a thick chunk of gammon.

"Let me have a good Sunday afternoon snooze, old boy, and then we will go for a nice walk before the evening service."

Caleb had a good snooze, a good walk, and a good evening service, and the next day, he was back to his normal, cheerful self. The sun shone, the sky was blue, the birds sang, and a light breeze made for a pleasant working day. Caleb whistled as he did his morning chores. During the short break between the arable harvests and apple picking, he and Matthew had agreed to help each other sort out the fat lambs from the two flocks for the market. Some jobs were easier to share.

At the appointed time, Caleb knocked on the Griffens' back door and entered, but immediately, he sensed something was wrong and felt like an intruder. Matthew and Lydia were sitting still and silent at the kitchen table. Lydia had obviously been crying, and Matthew sat despairingly with his head in his hand.

"Sorry, I barged in."

"You didn't. I said 'Come in,'" Lydia contradicted.

"I'll come back another time."

"Oh, the fat lambs!" sighed Matthew. "I had forgotten."

"No, no, don't worry." Caleb lifted the door latch, "We can do that another time."

"Stop, lad!" commanded Matthew, then muttered, as if to himself, "If ever we needed fat lamb money, it is now!"

Caleb stood in the doorway, feeling puzzled and awkward.

"Show him the letter, Lydia. The boy may as well know the situation."

Without looking up, Lydia slid the letter along the kitchen table. Caleb pulled out a chair, sat down, and picked up the letter.

Dear Mr and Mrs Griffen,

Circumstances have forced me to inform you of an unwelcome turn of events within my household and business. For the last three years, I have trained up your son, John, in my trade as a wheelwright as if he were my own. He was fed at my table and fared well. Despite all the goodwill my wife and I have shown him, he has, under our very noses, betrayed our trust by attempting to woo our daughter, Charlotte. How long this unfortunate understanding has been brewing, we cannot ascertain, but it is not a relationship we condone or wish to encourage.

Charlotte has complied with the wishes of my wife and I and has agreed to end the friendship, but John appears unrepentant and unmovable. The situation makes it impossible for him to stay under our roof. He has broken the covenant of his indentureship. John has been a diligent apprentice and is now a skilled wheelwright with only a few techniques to master. Although deeply grieved and vexed at his treatment of us, I was loath to dismiss John and sever his indenture. Therefore, I have found another Master Wheelwright in the neighbouring town of Woodbridge who is willing to take on your son for his final year despite his misdemeanour and stubborn attitude. However, the gentleman's indenture fees are considerably higher than mine. He will advise you of the monthly cost by letter.

As for my business, although I could not have offered your son a position long-term, I have invested a considerable amount of time in his training and have only just started reaping the benefits of it. I also must seek a new apprentice; therefore, I feel compelled to charge you half our contracted indenture fee for the next six months.

Yours faithfully

Geoffrey Mannering

Caleb read the letter, all the while feeling uncomfortable at prying so intimately into his friends' business and heartache.

"Oh dear!" was his somewhat inadequate conclusion as he finished.

"Indeed!" sighed Matthew.

"Has John ever hinted at this?" asked Caleb.

"Not a word," replied Lydia.

"He hardly ever writes, at the best of times," added Matthew.

"We don't blame Mr Mannering," Lydia stated. "He has been very generous to John—finding him a new position and all that." Her eyes were filling up again.

"It's John we are grieved with." Matthew's voice trembled with sorrow and anger. "He was never good at acknowledging his faults."

They all sat in glum silence.

"Where we find the extra money from is anyone's guess!" croaked Matthew.

Caleb's feeling of awkwardness rose to a whole new level. *The subject of personal finance, especially financial woes, is such a British taboo.*

"I can take on more dressmaking. Elsie can leave school to help me if necessary," Lydia suggested.

Matthew sat unresponsive, with his head still in his hands.

"I am so thankful that Suzie is so generous with her wages!" continued Lydia, attempting brightness. "You know, she hardly keeps a penny for herself."

"That's kind," acknowledged Caleb. *If she becomes Mrs Mortimer, her wages will be stopped.*

Silence fell again. Caleb wracked his brain to think of how he could help his dear neighbours. He was almost skint himself, so financial help was impossible.

"You know, I am willing to help in any way I can on your farm, don't you?" he offered wholeheartedly.

Lydia's eyes overflowed with tears as she touched his forearm.

"You are a tremendous help, dear Caleb. We are so thankful for you," she sobbed.

Matthew blew his nose loudly.

"Shall I make us all a pot of tea?" suggested Caleb.

Matthew pushed back his chair and stood up. "Drinking tea isn't going to get the lambs sorted, is it? No, lad, we had best get cracking and find some fat lambs with 'Wheelwright Indentureship' written on them." Smiling wryly at his dark joke, both men headed out the door to begin work.

CHAPTER 20

Suzie smiled and chatted brightly with Pru and Connie as she cut out the chain of paper men, but inside, she felt awkward and uncomfortable. Instead of being safely shut up in his study, Mr Mortimer spent the evening in the dining room with her and the girls. He did not add much to the conversation, but his presence spoilt the whole atmosphere. The girls were slightly on edge and subdued. She felt judged and found wanting, but even worse than that, Mr Mortimer seemed to stare at her. She knew it, even when she had her back turned to him.

Ever since the seaside holiday, their father had spent more time with the girls. He had accompanied them on walks, read stories to them on Sunday afternoons, and even eaten some meals with them. Suzie wondered if he felt guilty about pulling out of the holiday at the last minute. It was an excellent thing that he was spending more time with his daughters. Suzie did not want to intrude upon their family time and tried to gradually extract herself from the scene, but Mr Mortimer was having none of that. Her presence seemed vital.

She squirmed inside when he tried so earnestly, yet failed miserably, to be playful and humorous with the girls. She recoiled inside when he smiled, almost beseechingly, at her. She chided herself for her involuntary reactions—the poor man had suffered so deeply when his dear wife had died. He was only just beginning to recover. It was good that he was trying to reintroduce himself to everyday life again. She should try to help him rather than wish him back in his sorrowful study.

His behaviour yesterday in chapel was most odd. They always sat with the girls between them. Connie relied on her to follow the reading with her finger. The pew had never felt so short. After every hymn, Mr Mortimer seemed to sit down an inch closer to her. Suzie shuffled up the seat, gradually squashing herself up to the pew's unyielding wooden armrest, but still felt uncomfortably close to him. Suzie could hardly concentrate on the sermon as she held herself small and rigid . She cringed inside as she wondered what others might think. She pitied little Connie, so far away, needing her shoulder to lean on or her knee to doze on. Maybe he thought it was time for Connie to grow up a bit, or perhaps the sun was in his eyes at the other end of the pew. Whatever it was, she hoped it would not happen again next week. Did the sun shine through different windows at different times, depending on the year's seasonal cycle? Suzie wasn't sure. Anyway, maybe next Sunday would be overcast. Farmers often prayed for rainy Sundays during the summer—a good soaking on a day they were not working anyway. But probably this was the first time anyone had ever prayed for rain because of seating positions on a pew, Suzie thought wryly.

The evening hours seemed to drag, but eventually, it was the girls' bedtime, and Suzie had an excuse to escape with them upstairs. Once they were settled, Suzie reluctantly returned to the small dining room. She was relieved to find it empty. Of course, the room belonged to Mr Mortimer, but that fact did not stop Suzie from feeling as if he was trespassing when he entered. She had a few more chores to do before bedtime, including giving him an evening drink. At least he was back in his study—*like a jack-in-a-box, safely boxed in with the lid on*, she thought.

The next day, having taken the girls to Mrs Dillerstone (who did not recognise traditional school holidays), Suzie shut the front door with a huge sigh of relief. At last, she and Maggie had the house to themselves. She whistled as she flung open the windows and made the beds. If she hurried through the chores, maybe she might slip home for a few hours tomorrow. Invigorated by that thought, she flew through her tasks.

"You've gotta spring in ya step this morning," observed Maggie when they sat together for coffee.

"I want to get a lot done today so that I can pop home tomorrow for a few hours," Suzie explained.

"Oh, so no other reason?" questioned Maggie archly.

"Other reason? What like? Being pleased to have the girls back at school or something?"

"I were thinking more of their father."

"You what?" retorted Suzie sharply.

"It is clear to all te see that he has taken a shine te ya."

"No! Please not!" Suzie was horrified.

"Ya should be pleased. Ya're lucky to get his attention."

"I don't want his, so-called attention. I really don't."

"Why ever not? He's got a lot te offer. Ya'd live comfortably."

"But I don't like him, let alone love him," whimpered Suzie in distress.

Maggie snorted. "Whoever said that romantics were for the likes of us? '*I don't love him*!'" she mocked in a falsetto voice.

"I'd never be happy in a marriage with someone I didn't love," remonstrated Suzie.

"Since when did love and happiness put food on the table?" Suzie had never seen Maggie so vocal and forceful. "Imagine how much it would help ya folks, having ya wed above ya station. They want it. And as for ya, ya'd never 'ave te live 'and te mouth, like ya parents or us! No more 'ard work!"

"I'd prefer hard work with someone I love than a bed of roses with some miserable Mortimer man!" Suzie was upset and angry.

Maggie snorted even louder; she was looking upset herself. "Ya've read too many silly novels. Let me be clear: beggars can't be choosers."

"I am not a beggar. And I can be a chooser."

"There's no room in our world fa spinsters."

"I'll take the risk; thank you very much," retorted Suzie as she flounced out of the room.

Now, Suzie's day had been completely wrecked! Instead of breezing through her chores with a spring in her step, she crashed and slammed through them as if they were to blame. Everything that Maggie had said was disturbing, but worst of all was her confirming the inkling Suzie had been repressing. She had hoped that if she ignored her intuition long enough, the problem might go away, but it definitely did not. And would her parents really welcome such a match? Did they really want her off their hands? Would they think she was selfish if she rejected Mr Mortimer's offer?

What foolish thinking! He hadn't made an offer, and hopefully, he never would. But what would her parents want? Questions whirled around and around her head until they pounded. Why was life so complicated? Suddenly, the Mortimers' smart townhouse felt like a constricted cage. Suzie was a prowling, agitated lion, longing to escape and run to the open fields and countryside.

Suzie was in no mood for fun crafts or games that evening, but neither were the girls. They were fractious and argumentative after a stifling day in Mrs Dillerstone's forbidding presence. The only thing that kept the evening from being truly awful was that Mr Mortimer was delayed at work. Making an excuse to herself that the girls needed fresh air and exercise, Suzie bundled them out the front door and escaped with them for a long walk. A long, long walk! Long enough to make a fireside with father session impossible. Poor Prue and Connie were exhausted and hungry by the time they returned home. Suzie hastily stoked them up with milk and biscuits before marching them to bed. Feeling slightly pleased with herself that she had avoided one undesirable situation, yet knowing she couldn't be sure that Jack was firmly in his box, Suzie cautiously entered her dining room. The room was empty—she let out a sigh of relief. Opening the stove, she saw that, too, was empty—he had taken out his congealed, kept-warm supper. All she now needed to do was make him his milky evening drink and disappear to bed.

Suzie knocked on Mr Mortimer's study door, briskly removed his empty plate, and replaced it with his drink.

"Good night, sir," she muttered as she headed for the door.

"Suzannah, stay a moment." Her heart sank to the soles of her boots.

Mr Mortimer rose from his chair and waved his hand towards the visitor's chair.

"Do take a seat."

At this unprecedented move, Suzie's mind went swiftly to a poem she had learnt at school:

"Will you walk into my parlour?" said a spider to a fly;

"'Tis the prettiest little parlour that ever you did spy.

The way into my parlour is up a winding stair,

And I have many pretty things to shew when you are there."

"Oh no, no!" said the little fly, "to ask me is in vain,

For who goes up your winding stair can ne'er come down again."

Don't be so mean. If Maggie hadn't planted such stupid ideas in your brain, you wouldn't be thinking so nastily about him. Suzie chided herself.

A long silence filled the room.

"The girls went back to Mrs Dillerstone's today," offered Suzie to pierce the strained silence.

"Very good."

"We went for a long walk afterwards to get their energy off."

Suzie studies the carpet. The strange swirling pattern looked like a line of disapproving eyes.

"They are very fond of you, Suzannah."

"That's nice."

The line of eyes mocked her. Although she studied the carpet, she knew Mr Mortimer's eyes were also on her. He cleared his throat.

"Suzannah, I would like you to marry me."

Suzie stared hard at the hateful row of eyes—they were spiders' eyes.

She opened her mouth to protest, but he raised his hand.

"Now, Suzannah, hear me out. You would make me a very suitable wife. My daughters are flourishing under your supervision. You are honest and hardworking and seem like a God-fearing young lady. My offer can raise you, and more indirectly, your family, out of poverty. I can elevate you to a position far above that which you were born into." Then, as if laying down his trump card, he said, "I have prayed long and hard about the situation, and I strongly believe this is the right thing for both of us."

"What if I don't think it is the right thing?"

Mr Mortimer smiled at her benevolently. "Then maybe you need to pray for submission."

Suzie mumbled inarticulately and stood up. As she stumbled out of the room, she thought he said something like, "Take as long as you need to see sense, my dear."

My dear! Suzie felt repulsed and trapped. She could be the fly that got away, couldn't she?

Suzie ran upstairs.

Laying in bed, staring at the ceiling, Suzie thought of everything she should have said: She was far too young for him. She didn't love him. She had no great desire to be elevated above the position she was born into. She would not marry him! Never ever!

The next morning, feeling sleep-deprived and desperate to escape, Suzie was determined to visit her parents. She needed a listening ear and some sound advice. She dropped the girls off at Mrs Dillerstone's and headed straight for home. The household chores could wait. Maggie could get alarmed; Mr Mortimer could get annoyed. She didn't mind. In fact, she wanted him to.

Leaving the town behind her, she marched along the quiet country lanes. She had no time to dawdle and admire the hedgerows. She needed to be back later to pick up the girls. They should not be allowed to suffer. With every step, Suzie's certainty wobbled into uncertainty. Was she just being selfish? Was it right to put her needs before those of the girls? Those of a respected deacon? Maybe those of her family? Hadn't she asked the Lord Jesus to be her Saviour and King of her life? Was being Mrs Mortimer God's plan for her? Many people had given up more than romantic dreams for the Lord. Missionaries go away from home, and loved ones at His command. Martyrs were willing to give up life itself for their Lord.

And what about her family? Was she a financial burden and a worry to them? She didn't think so. She gave almost all her wages to her mother, who was always most grateful for them. She was far less of a burden on them than John. But what if she refused Mr Mortimer? Would he dismiss her? She stopped short. She hadn't considered that aspect of the situation.

What would happen to Prue and Connie? They would be heartbroken if she was dismissed. They would make wonderful stepdaughters. She knew she had brightened up their grey little lives.

And what about Mr Mortimer himself? His grief had been great. Surely, he loved his wife intently to mourn so deeply. Maybe there was a wonderful side to him she was yet to discover. Suzie shuddered; even if there was a hidden side to him, she did not want to find it out.

But there I go, being self-centred again!

Between every new thought that ran through her brain and every thought that repeated itself, Suzie prayed earnestly, "Please show me what to do."

CHAPTER 21

Lydia flew through her morning chores. The quicker she did them, the more time she would have for sewing. Matthew often made snide and belittling comments about her sideline, which was hurtful. It was probably his male pride being hurt, she decided. Being the main breadwinner was so important for men. But he didn't seem to mind the extra savings in their jam jars. The letter from Mr Mannering had hit them both hard. It had knocked Matthew straight back into the deep, dark hole he had been slowly emerging from. The family were once again treading on eggshells. Lydia was trying to be sympathetic, but it was difficult. They were all affected by the news, not just him. Feeling sorry for yourself was not going to cure the situation. Positive action was needed, and that is exactly what Lydia had done. Unbeknownst to her husband, she had written to Gwendoline, asking for the names of suppliers of second-hand sewing machines. Lydia could only imagine how much more work she could get through if she owned such a machine. All the tedious long seams could be so quickly and neatly stitched in a fraction of the time. Also, this is how other businesses operate. To be competitive, she needed to keep up with the times. Of course, some jam jar money would need to be used to invest in the machine, but Matthew should be used to that concept—you spend hard-earned money buying good seed as an investment for a harvest. The chances of a good return on a sewing machine seemed rather higher than on seed; at least, the weather, insects, and disease didn't come into the equation. Flooding the market didn't seem to be a problem either. Everyone needed to wear clothes, thanks to Adam and Eve, and all clothes wear out. No one else in the village seemed remotely interested in becoming her rival. She didn't know much about the bull and bear markets...

Lydia's thoughts were interrupted by the back door flying open and Suzie greeting her with a hug and kiss.

"What a wonderful surprise!" beamed Lydia.

Suzie filled up the kettle and put it on the stove. "I couldn't wait any longer to see you all and get up to date with all your news."

I must definitely not tell her about John. She will only want to give even more of her wages, thought Lydia as she floured the kitchen table to knead bread dough.

As she kneaded half of the lump, Suzie chatted about this and that, but Lydia sensed she was not herself.

"Are you okay, Suzie? Has something happened?"

Suzie thumped the dough hard. "Mr Mortimer has asked me to marry him."

This was not what Lydia had expected.

"Oh! And what do you think about that?"

The floodgates opened.

"I do not want to marry him! But am I just being self-centred?" Thump. "The girls really need me." Thump! "Mr Mortimer thinks it is the Lord's will." Thump. "He says it would ease your burdens." Thump. "I don't want to live in a posh place like that." Thump. "I don't even like him." THUMP. "I want to do the right thing."

"Spare a thought for the dough!" Lydia deftly exchanged lumps.

"Ma, this is serious!"

"Yes, I know, dear. There is a lot to think about. But, first, you don't like him nor want to marry him. That is it then—discussion ended."

"But is it? What if I am supposed to marry him?"

"If the Lord wanted you to be his wife, He would put that desire in your heart."

The cat, who had been around their feet, walked to the back door and meowed loudly. With a deft skill performed many times, Lydia undid the catch with her wrist, not her floury hands, and opened the door. The sun beamed brightly, and she left the door open. Returning to her work, Lydia continued,

"I don't think the Lord would ever make someone marry someone they did not love."

"What about Esther?"

Lydia didn't know what to say. "Well, now, that is a difficult one. God was overruling a very pagan king and a very pagan decree for His own good and the preservation of His people. I don't think your situation is anywhere near that." Another thought came to her: "God's relationship to His people is primarily of love, not duty. Any duty we do should spring from love. The Pharisees did duty but not love." This was a huge subject; it needed thinking through.

"Am I just being selfish? The girls need a bit of fun and love in their lives."

"Yes, but if you married him against your will, you would be miserable, and that would make their life miserable too."

"Would you be relieved if I married a rich man?"

"Not unless you were happy."

"I wouldn't be. I would rather marry someone penny-less who I loved," Suzie stoutly declared, "and work myself to the bone than marry a rich man I didn't like. Money can't make you happy. I'd rather...."

Lydia caught a movement in the corner of her eye, and before she knew it, Caleb had walked into the kitchen. Everyone froze and felt awkward.

"I beg your pardon for interrupting," stammered Caleb. "I had agreed to meet Matthew here."

"Suzie has paid us a surprise visit; isn't that nice?" gushed Lydia. She glanced at her daughter, who looked flustered.

"Yes, it is nice to be home for a few hours," she commented inanely.

"Yes, especially with the sun shining," replied Caleb, ignoring that the sun had shone nicely nearly all summer. He twisted his cap in his hand.

"Well, I had better look elsewhere for Matthew. Sorry to disturb you, ladies. Good day."

They listened to his retreating footsteps.

"He must have heard all of that!" wailed Suzie.

"So what!?" Lydia replied, "No one will think worse of you for those wise sentiments."

"What wise sentiments?" asked Matthew, appearing from the front room in his outdoor boots.

Now was not the time to go into all the ins and outs of the conversation. "Suzie was just saying it is far better to marry for love than for money."

"Humph," growled Matthew, "fine sentiments indeed, but love doesn't put bread on the table, does it? Now, where is that, Caleb?"

"He's just been to the back door."

"I've been standing there, twiddling my thumbs at the front gate, waiting for him. He knew the tree to fell was along the lane, not on the farm." He stormed out the back door, muttering about the youth of today.

"Pa a bit snarly again?"

"I'm afraid so," admitted Lydia with a sigh.

"Anything in particular set him off?" Suzie asked.

Lydia longed to confide in her eldest daughter, who was becoming wise and thoughtful.

"The general stresses and strains of everyday life, I suppose," she replied vaguely.

All too soon, it was time for Suzie to return to Milford—the girls needed collecting from Mrs Dillerstone at three o'clock. Suzie lost her bounce and sparkle as she prepared to leave.

"Oh, my Suzie girl, I wish I could come with you and face Mr Mortimer for you!"

Suzie sighed. "That would be nice, but I am a grown-up now, aren't I?"

"I can't be with you, but I can pray for you."

"And I really appreciate that!" Suzie nodded earnestly.

Lydia hugged her tightly and said, "Stay strong in your resolve to say no."

"I'll try," Suzie answered weakly.

As Lydia waved her daughter off from the garden gate and watched her disappear down the lane, she thought about the many times she had watched her go off to school. Little did she know then that waving goodbye would only get harder. Little worries about little children become big worries about big children. She was grateful that she had a big God to commit all her concerns to.

CHAPTER 22

The afternoon was far too hot for brisk walking, but hurry, she must, if she was going to be in time to collect the girls. An inelegant perspiration may have been acceptable in Brookfield but had no place in Milford. Thinking about it, Suzie realised she even walked differently in the two places. At home, in her rough clothes, wooden clogs, and loosened corset, she took big, purposeful strides with a relaxed arm swing. In Milford, clad in fashionable dresses fitting snugly over properly strung-up corsets and wearing narrow lace-up boots, Suzie walked with a rigid back and small steps. It reminded Suzie of the description of the daughters of Zion in Isaiah chapter three:

"Because the daughters of Zion are haughty and walk with stretched forth necks and wanton eyes, walking and mincing as they go, and making a tinkling with their feet."

At least she didn't tinkle with her feet or wanton eyes!!

But much to her relief, Suzie did not have to stride or mince her way to Milford. Mr Green drew alongside her with his horse and cart and offered her a lift.

"I's on te way te Milford, ma gal, so 'op on."

Suzie hopped on gratefully.

"I 'eared about ya, and ya troubles with Mr Biggs at te big 'ouse."

"Yes, I didn't last long there, did I?" Suzie laughed wryly.

"'E's a rouge, that man. I 'ope 'e soon gets 'is comeuppance".

"That would be nice," agreed Suzie. "And how are the greenhouses and kitchen gardens at the big house doing this season?"

That was all she needed to ask for the duration of the journey. With great detail and enthusiasm, Mr Green expounded on the abundance and variety of salad vegetables sent to the kitchens. After giving some exact figures in pounds and ounces (far excelling last year's bounty), he moved on to the vexing subject of green fly and extolled various methods and theories of prevention and eradication (none of which were totally fly-proof).

After being dropped off at the Prince Albert Memorial Fountain, Suzie scurried through the streets to the Mortimer residence. She would have time for a quick drink of cold water and five minutes to herself before needing to head out to Mrs Dillerstone's.

Instead of finding a quiet, empty house, she was greeted by wails and exclamations. Prue nose-dived into Suzie's skirt, "Oh, I am so pleased you are still alive!" Hard on her heels was a pale and tearful Connie, holding a blood-soaked hankie to her nose. Suzie bent down, hugged them both, and planted kisses in their hair.

"Whatever has happened?" she asked as she herded them into the little sitting room.

A grim-faced Maggie awaited her there.

"Wherever have you been?" she demanded accusingly. "We've had a right old drama here. I've had to stay on late."

"Connie had a nosebleed at Mrs Dillerstone's. It wouldn't stop. Her maid ran to get you, but you weren't here," wailed Prue. "I thought she would bleed to death!"

"And you weren't here to look after me!" sobbed Connie, and with that, the bleeding restarted, and Connie panicked. "It will never ever stop!" she blubbered, pressing her teary, blooded face further into Suzie's shoulder.

Suzie had never dealt with this sort of crisis before, but she couldn't give any impression of uncertainty. She had seen her mother deal with various calamities. Sending off an arrow prayer, she sprang into action.

"Connie dear, come and lay your head on my knee and let me pinch the top of your nose. Maggie, can you please see if any of the neighbours have some ice we can use? Prue, can you go and get your sister a nice, clean hankie from the top drawer of your bedroom chest of drawers?"

Maggie and Prue scattered.

Connie retched and spat out blood.

Suzie thought quickly—laying down wasn't working. Despite Connie looking so pale, she needed to sit up and lean forward. Still holding her firmly by the nose, Suzie sat her on her lap and leaned forward.

"You're hurting my nose," whimpered Connie.

"I'm sorry, my dear. I need to." With her other hand, Suzie rubbed Connie's arm reassuringly. *"Please, Lord, stop the bleeding fast."*

"I can't find the hankie draw!" shouted Prue over the bannister.

"Top left-hand draw," Suzie shouted back.

"Which is left?"

"Put both your hands in front of you and put out your thumbs. The hand with the thumb making an L the right way around is your left," yelled Suzie.

"Which way around is a L?"

"Oh, don't worry. Just get me a dishcloth from the kitchen."

Maggie came panting back, bearing a huge chunk of ice.

"We only need a little block. Can you carve off a bit?" Suzie asked.

"I don't know which knife to use."

Suzie let out an exasperated sigh. "Try any you can lay your hands on. Maybe the meat knife?"

Meanwhile, Connie was beginning to feel cold and clammy. Suzie pressed harder. Connie whimpered.

111

A shout came from the kitchen. "Ouch, I've just cut meself! The knife slid off the ice."

Suzie's heart sank further. "Wrap it up and carry on. Please!!" she begged.

After more huffing and puffing from the kitchen, Maggie emerged with a huge bandage on her finger and a tiny piece of ice. *How can one hold ice to a little nose and pinch it at the same time?* Suzie asked herself. Somehow, she managed. Finally, just as Suzie was about to summon the doctor, the bleeding stopped. Suzie felt weak with relief. Gently laying her patient on the sofa, she went to get her a tepid drink. She knew it mustn't be either too hot or too cold. She cradled Connie's head in her arms as she gave her sips.

"Please don't leave me, Suzie," pleaded Connie.

Suzie smiled lovingly at the little girl. "I'll sit on the sofa. Put your head on my lap, like so, and have a good long sleep. I won't leave you." She stroked her hair soothingly.

"Maggie," she called softly towards the kitchen, "what about a nice pot of tea for you and me? I think it will be just the ticket. And I think the girls could have something from the sweetie jar."

Maggie grumbled. "I suppose being home even later won't make no difference."

"You deserve a good cuppa," Suzie tried to sound reconciliatory.

Before the tea tray or sweetie jar had appeared, Connie was fast asleep, and Prue was playing happily with her dolls' house.

For a while, they sat in silence, sipping at their tea. Maggie kept her bandaged hand elevated to her chest as if it were a life-threatening injury. The only noises were the gentle, blocked-nose-sounding snores of Connie and Prue softly carrying out a conversation between two dolls in their house.

"Why did you disappear this morning?" hissed Maggie quietly. "It was most irresponsible!"

Suzie had to agree. She should have told Maggie about her plan. The urge to rush home had been too overwhelming, but that was no excuse.

"I'm sorry. I shouldn't have behaved like that."

"You caused no end of alarm to the girls—and me."

"I'm sorry. I won't do that again."

Silence again reigned, and Suzie was left with her own thoughts. How selfishly she had acted! How much the dear little girls needed her! Gloom enveloped her. It had all seemed so simple: back in the farmhouse kitchen, declaring she would not marry Mr Mortimer. But now? She stroked Connie's blond hair lovingly. What if she poured all her love and affection onto her daughters, not her husband? Would that work? Would a man like Mr Mortimer, who liked his own company so much, even notice her lack of ardour? What was the minimum a wife could offer? In the epistles, men were commanded to love their wives, but women were only told to reverence their husbands. She might manage reverence better than love.

Maggie went home, Prue continued to play happy families in the dolls' house, and Connie slept peacefully as Suzie sat perfectly still, feeling wretched, confused, and trapped. Her head throbbed with conflicting thoughts. Every time the innocent, vulnerable little girl on her knee stirred, a chain of selfless duty coiled tighter around Suzie's heart. The girls needed her, and that trumped everything else.

The image of her parent's young and sun-tanned neighbour flitted through her mind's eye. His windswept hair, muscular forearms, ready smile, and kindly manner. She swiftly dismissed the painful image. A tear rolled down her cheeks. Some things in life are not meant to be. She should grow out of romantic nonsense and face the real world. Even her father seemed to have poo-poo romantic sentimentality, and she respected his opinion. An awful thought suddenly struck her—she had always assumed her parents' marriage was based on love. What if it wasn't? It felt as if the bottom was falling out of her world.

Prue came and had another sweet from the jar, then happily returned to her game. Suzie continued to sit. Maybe if she did the right thing and married Mr Mortimer (even the words made her shudder), God would reward her by giving her love to him. Maybe it would grow and blossom. Miracles can happen. If not love, maybe at least affection—that wasn't too much to ask for. Was it?

The afternoon turned to evening, and still, Connie slept on. Suzie gently extracted herself from the sofa, placed a cushion under Connie's head, and prepared tea for Prue. She, herself, had no appetite. The thought of seeing Mr Mortimer later only added to her gloom. Feigning jollity for poor Prue's sake, Suzie cut the sandwiches into animal shapes. As they ate a

113

hushed meal, Prue explained all that her doll family had been doing that afternoon.

When Connie finally woke up, she was pale but in good spirits. She ate a hearty supper and drank plenty of milk. With extremely mixed motives, Suzie decided she should devote her whole evening to the ongoing care of her little patient. She wrote a note to Mr Mortimer, explaining that she needed to constantly watch poor Connie after a severe nosebleed and would thus be occupied the entire evening. His supper was being kept warm in the stove; she hoped he enjoyed it.

Little did Mr Mortimer realise, bunkered down in his study, that, far from watching his daughter languish on a bed of affliction, Suzie's main occupation that evening was calming the over-excited patient down and trying to prevent her from bashing her tender little nose again.

Whether from a wholehearted concern for Connie, or to appease her guilt for being absent earlier, or to prove to herself she had a water-tight reason for avoiding Mr Mortimer, or a mixture of all the above, Suzie slept the night on the girls' bedroom floor. She wondered about other people as she lay on the hard, makeshift bed. Did they have such difficulty in understanding their motives? Some people (especially those in the chapel) looked so wholesome and good. It was hard to imagine that they did anything for dubious or mixed motives. Maybe (hopefully), she also looked unquestionably wholesome. But it troubled her that, if one were to dig deep into even her best actions, from her best motives, somewhere in the spade-load of goodness, there would be, at the very least, a tiny seam of selfishness, pride, or some other obnoxious trait. She felt worse and more complicated than everyone else. Then she remembered the apostle Paul's groan: "When I would do good, evil is present with me." And "Oh, wretched man that I am!" Suzie eased herself into a more comfortable position. She was so thankful that salvation was a free and complete gift and not earned by works.

CHAPTER 23

Suzie slept fitfully. The cushions she had bound together with a sheet to make a mattress kept going in different directions, leaving her on the hard floorboards. Connie and Prue's gentle snores were sweet and cosy but they did little to steel her resolve to say no. To be or not to be Mrs Mortimer, that is the question. By the morning, Suzie came to the reluctant conclusion that she would say yes for the good of others. Maybe, once the uncertainty was taken away, she would probably feel better and become more positive. Seeing the girls' excitement at having a new mama would probably help propel her towards positivity. On the thorny subject of motives, was it possible to do the wrong thing for the right motives? Suzie stopped herself. She must stop overthinking the problems and just get on with it.

The normal breakfast routine, thankfully, took over her thoughts, and she busied herself with the girls. Connie had bounced back so remarkably that she was fit enough to go to Mrs Dillerstone's—much to Prue's relief (who would want to go there alone?) and Connie's disappointment.

Having waved goodbye to the girls and had coffee with Maggie, Suzie decided to escape the house and go on a few errands. A book needed to go to the bookbinders. She needed a new carpet brush from the hardware store and a pair of Mr Mortimer's shoes needed collecting from the cobbler. It was so good to get out into the town and mingle. The book was handed over, and the brush was bought. All that remained was a trip to the cobbler. Suzie had never been there, as Maggie had taken them, but she soon found the little workshop. A bell jingled as she opened the door. A pleasant aroma of leather, oil, and polish welcomed her. She felt as if she had stepped into Aladdin's cave. Rows of boots and shoes lined the wall, and a huge array of tools, leather, and wood were scattered over the floor. A small, thin man was busy sewing a pair of boots by a window in the far corner. Before Suzie could fully take in the scene, a rotund woman came descending a narrow set of stairs, which creaked and complained with every step. She seemed to fill the already-crowded room.

"And how may I help you?" she demanded.

"I have come to pick up a pair of shoes, please."

"Name?"

"Mortimer."

"Humph," snorted the woman as she sorted through a shelf of finished shoes. "Mr Humphrey Mortimer!"

"Yes, that is right," agreed Suzie, thinking it was a question.

"Mr Humphrey Mortimer!" The shoes were slammed onto the counter. "Do you know the man?" she asked, fixing Suzie with an intense stare.

"Well, yes," stammered Suzie. "I help to look after his daughters."

"That man killed my best friend."

The woman looked so angry. Suzie took a step backwards. She imagined the huge woman picking her up with one arm and flinging her out of the shop. For the first time, the man in the corner glanced up from his work.

"Oh?" replied Suzie weakly.

"Did you ever know Mrs Martha Mortimer—the girls' late mother?"

"No."

"Well, poor dear Martha was my best friend. Full of joy, fun, and youth. Mr Mortimer set his cap on her and wouldn't take no for an answer. Would he, Fred? The man wore her down with his badgering. He used every argument he could think of. Oh, he would raise her beyond her station in life. She would have a lovely house and live like a lady, but none of that

116

moved Martha. No one could accuse her of being materialistic." The woman glared at Suzie as if she might dare to try.

"But then, poor Martha buckled. The cold-hearted Mortimer started persuading her that it was her religious duty to marry him—her destined path. Sweet Martha was a good, simple soul who wanted to do the right thing. Before we knew it, he had marched her down the aisle. Isn't that right, Fred?"

If Fred responded at all, Suzie had blinked at the time.

"Well, that was the end of the Martha we knew. She got her fine house and probably lived like a lady, but a solitary lady. He worked all hours but never let her out. He never let her visit her friends. He despised her family, and he belittled her. Isn't that the truth, Fred?"

Fred nodded slightly.

The woman smacked the shoes onto the counter again.

"I've never seen a woman shrivel inside so much. I reckon her only joys were her faith and her darling daughters. His mean, cold demeanour sapped her of life, and she died of a fairly mild illness. Too worn out to resist. Wasn't she, Fred?"

Fred grunted.

"That is tragic!" gasped Suzie.

"Awful," agreed the woman, her double chin shaking with emotion. "And from what I hear, he has tried to catch other poor girls in the same way—wearing them down with sanctimonious arguments. Haven't we heard that, Fred?"

"Aye." Fred was waxing lyrical.

Suzie paid the bill and took the shoes.

"Thank you very much for your help today. I really appreciate it and am deeply indebted to you," she said as she left, leaving the cobbler's wife amazed at such gratitude for resoling shoes.

That evening, Mr Mortimer was late home due to a deacon's meeting. As soon as Suzie knew he was settled in his study, she warmed up his milk and water bedtime beverage, steeled herself, and marched into his lair. She handed him his drink.

"Mr Mortimer, I have made my final decision. I will not marry you." Suzie was agreeably surprised by how calm and resolute her voice sounded.

Instead of slumping with disappointment, Mr Mortimer straightened up in anger.

"So, you are defying my expressed wishes?" he challenged.

"I am."

"And wilfully rejecting the right path to take?"

This was too much for Suzie to stomach.

"The right path, indeed?" she snorted scornfully. "I can't imagine a more wrong path—marrying a man I don't love? Being enticed by status and possessions, and having my arm twisted by spiritual blackmail?"

Mr Mortimer opened his mouth to speak, but Suzie continued.

"I love your daughters. They need a mother, but it will never be me!" There was far more she could say, but she decided against it.

"Then you are not the woman I thought you to be," he said condemningly.

"No, I am not."

"Your willfulness makes you most unsuitable."

"Very unsuitable indeed," she wholeheartedly agreed.

She turned to leave the room.

"And you are dismissed—with immediate effect!"

Suzie swung around again.

"Mr Mortimer, that is not a wise plan." She now spoke slowly and calmly, as if reasoning with a child. "Your daughters have experienced a terrible loss. If I disappear from their little lives overnight, it may have a very detrimental effect on them."

Mr Mortimer looked thoughtful. Suzie sat on the spare chair opposite him.

"Let me stay for one week. We will prepare them for my departure. You can seek out a replacement for me. I could even stay until you find one, if you prefer. Your daughters need to know they are always welcome at the farm. Maybe they can even come and stay for a few nights during their holidays. I do not just want to disappear. They must not be damaged by our disagreement."

Mr Mortimer sat motionless. Suzie almost felt sorry for him.

"One week."

"One week," agreed Suzie, and she fled the room before he could change his mind.

CHAPTER 24

Caleb watched with concern as Matthew straightened himself up. Trimming sheep's feet was a backbreaking job for the youngest of farmers, let alone the likes of Mr Griffen. For several months now, they had run their flocks together. It made sense—neither of them had a huge number of sheep, and by amalgamating them, they could rotate the grazing more efficiently. Caleb also hoped that the arrangement would give Matthew less work to do.

He worried about his neighbour. Matthew was too proud and taciturn to say much, but how he walked and went about routine tasks made Caleb suspect he was in constant pain. If he thought no one was around, he often let out a groan and grimaced. When they worked together, Caleb often tried to do the donkey work and let Matthew have the lighter part. But that ploy was tricky. Caleb didn't want Matthew to feel patronised or as if he thought he was better at it than him. Today, Matthew seemed even quieter than usual and a little distracted.

Having finished trimming the fourth hoof of his ewe, Caleb rolled her over onto her feet. She staggered off, and he straightened up.

"I wonder if we have been a bit ambitious," he said, flexing his back to ease the ache. "Maybe we should do the rest tomorrow."

Twenty or so more ewes were in the holding pen, reluctantly waiting to be done.

"Then we'd have to keep them separated from the others 'cause we haven't marked the ones we've done," observed Matthew.

"True." There was nothing for it; they would have to continue. Caleb thought again.

"I don't know about yours, but my knife is getting a bit blunt."

"Aye, mine isn't too sharp either."

"I still haven't got my own grindstone. What if you sharpen yours, then I use it while you sharpen mine?"

Matthew nodded in agreement. "And I'll bring you back some cold tea if you like."

"Wonderful."

Spurred on by the success of his plan, Caleb ignored his protesting back and wrestled the next ewe to the floor. By the time both knives were sharp and two mugs of cold tea were fetched, there were only six more sheep in the pen.

"You've got a move on, lad," observed Matthew, climbing the hurdle into the pen.

"A sharp knife makes all the difference. Thanks."

Having finished the job and released the sheep into their meadow, the two men sat down. Leaning against the huge trunk of an old oak tree, they sipped their tea. Tish flopped down next to Caleb and put her head on his leg.

Matthew broke the silence.

"You know about the trouble with John, don't you?"

Caleb nodded, "Yes, very sad."

"Well, now it is our Suzie."

Caleb waited for a further explanation. It was long in coming.

Matthew drained his mug.

"She's got the sack. Mr Mortimer proposed; she declined, so he sacked her."

"Well, what a thing!" Caleb hoped the burst of joy he felt wasn't audible in his voice.

"She's got a week to get the girls used to the idea; she insisted on that. 'Tis all in a letter scribbled to us."

"That is sensible and kind. I think the girls are very fond of her."

"Yes, it will be a blow for them."

The afternoon sun played on their faces through the gently swaying leaves. Both were reluctant to move. Matthew flicked the tea dregs onto the ground.

"Problem is, we relied on her money."

Caleb nodded slowly. Matthew picked up a twig and started fiddling with it.

"And that's what I want to talk to you about."

Reaching for his pocketknife, he started whittling the stick.

Caleb squatted an ant that was crawling up his leg and waited.

"You see, lad, I'm not getting any younger. I don't relish the idea of another winter working out in all the elements."

Long curls of wood shavings fell to the grass. Caleb plucked a dock leaf and gently stripped the flesh from the veins.

"It'll probably take Suzie some time to lick her wounds and find a job. There aren't many jobs around for women in these parts unless you get employed by the big house, and she's blotted her copybook there. My thoughts are that I go and seek a job and leave her here to manage the farm for the winter months." Caleb rubbed Tish's nose lovingly.

"Do you think you could find a temporary job?" Caleb asked, picking up a second leaf. Tish nudged him with her nose, wondering why the tea break was lengthy.

"They want men for the extension of the railway track. I'll have to travel a bit down the line to find work. Most jobs would be outside, but some of them would be under canvas, at least."

122

"And how does Suzie feel about this?"

"I haven't mentioned it yet, but she will be delighted. She loves outdoor work. My Suzie is a grafter."

"What does Lydia think?"

Matthew shrugged guiltily. "I haven't discussed it with her. I wanted to sound you out first."

"Why me?" Caleb was surprised.

"Well, we're almost business partners, aren't we? I didn't want to suddenly land you with a novice to work with without getting your approval."

Caleb grinned. "I don't mind working with a novice."

"You'll keep your eye on her, won't you?"

"I promise I will."

"And make sure her business decisions are sound?"

"I'll try."

"I am most grateful."

"Not at all! You and Lydia have been so good to me."

"Humph!" dismissed Matthew as he heaved himself into a standing position.

"Where do you get pain, Matthew?"

"Who mentioned pain?" he sounded curt.

"No one. I just wondered. Farming takes its toll on the body."

"My back and hips aren't as quite as they used to be. They nag a bit," he admitted as he hobbled off to the next job.

Caleb whistled as he strolled back to the farm. He felt a surge of contentment. If he had to choose who he would like to work with throughout the winter, Suzie Griffen would definitely not be his last choice! He felt pretty sure that a new element of fun was about to enter his life. No one could accuse her of being dull! Suddenly, he checked himself—poor Matthew. "They ache a bit," which probably meant he was in constant pain! No wonder the poor man was sometimes a bit melancholy and terse. All that, plus the awful prospect ahead of him. He was going to leave his wife, children, and the only home he had ever known to seek work, competing with far younger men. Caleb pitied him. Was there any other solution that should be considered? He wracked his brain for ideas but found none. Anyway, telling his neighbour what to do was not his place. Matthew would not appreciate that. All he must do is support him in his decision. Caleb pondered. *People say money doesn't bring you happiness, and that's true. But money can certainly prevent lots of sadness.*

CHAPTER 25

Suzie had never been so grateful and relieved to see Mrs Marianne White as she was that Thursday. Less than forty-eight hours had passed since the conversation in the study, but so much had changed. Decisions had to be made, and Mr Mortimer's refusal to engage in direct conversation was not conducive to sensible planning.

Both girls rushed to the front door to greet their auntie and Thomas.

"You are not at Mrs Dillerstone's! Why ever not?" Suzie took her bonnet off and let the girls answer the question.

"We never have to go to her again!" Prue answered gleefully, jumping around in circles.

"Never, ever!" chimed in Connie.

Mrs White extracted herself from the three excited children and joined Suzie in the small dining room. "Now, Suzannah, please explain to me what is going on. Why are the girls not returning to Mrs D? And why are you leaving?"

Without pausing for a reply, she marched into the kitchen.

"Maggie, will you please take milk and biscuits to the children and supervise for a while? Suzannah, make us both a cup of coffee, then come and explain."

Maggie looked highly displeased at having her morning routine interrupted. As Suzie was getting the coffee ready, she whispered to her,

"Take your coffee along, too, so you don't miss out." Maggie snorted a reply. Since learning that Suzie had foolishly turned down Mr Mortimer's kind and generous offer, Maggie had been very offhand.

Once Maggie was out of earshot, Mrs White launched in.

"Right, Suzannah. I need some answers here. I am going to be the one left trying to sort out the problems, so you need to tell me all about it."

Suzie took a deep breath.

"Well, about Mrs Dillerstone. She became even more wheezy than usual yesterday and sent the girls home with her maid. Later in the day, we received a message that her physician had instructed her to have complete bed rest because her asthma had progressed from dormant to acute. She has decided to retire from tutoring."

"About time, too!" Mrs White declared, "I hated being taught by her. She seemed like an ancient relic even then. So, what are my brother's plans for the girls?"

Suzie shrugged, "I have no idea; he is not talking to me."

"Oh! How irritatingly childish of him!"

She sipped her coffee.

"And how have the girls taken the prospect of you leaving them?"

"I haven't told them," Suzie confessed.

"Why ever not?" Mrs White was annoyed. "You have less than five days left."

"Mr Mortimer is not talking, so I don't know his immediate plans for the girls. I wanted to speak to you before I told them so we could organise something."

Mrs White looked slightly mollified.

"Yes, I see it is awkward for you. I assume my brother proposed marriage to you?"

Suzie nodded.

"Very unsuitable," tutted Mrs White. Suzie wasn't sure if she disapproved of his actions or his choice of wife, but she saw no need for clarification.

Mrs White dunked a shortbread into her coffee. Suzie stared in horror at the action, knowing it had been submerged for far too long. The sodden end of the biscuit emerged, briefly plonked into the cup. Mrs White grabbed a teaspoon, retrieved the wayward morsel, and ate it.

"Right, this is my plan. The girls come and stay with me for a few weeks until Humphrey sorts out his staffing situation. On returning, they can attend the local school and make friends their own age instead of being mothballed up with an old dame."

Suzie stared at her with awe and gratitude.

"That would be perfect. They love staying with you, and going to school would be so nice for them." Being eager to please angelic-looking Milford girls, they would have no problems with Miss Maple.

Mrs White looked smug and helped herself to another biscuit.

"What would Mr Mortimer think of your schooling idea?" Suzie asked.

"Oh, I will manage that," Mrs White said, waving away any concerns with her cup. "He only sent them to Mrs D, as he felt some sort of loyalty to the old woman. Don't you worry, I will win this one."

Suzie was quite sure she would.

"And now we will call in the girls and tell them the plan."

Somehow, the bitter pill of Suzie's departure was so wrapped in the large spoonful of honey regarding staying at Thomas's house that the girls swallowed it without a tear. They wanted to start packing immediately. They couldn't wait to play in the big garden, be given rides in the wheelbarrow by friendly gardeners, play with Auntie's old dolls' house, or sing songs with the nursery nurse again. Oh, it would be lovely—all that richness on top of the wonderful realisation that they would never have another stuffy day at Mrs Dillerstone's dining room table, made the girls almost deliriously happy.

Happy, that is, until bedtime. As they were saying their evening prayers and climbing into bed, it suddenly dawned on them that life was about to change.

"Suzie, are you coming to Auntie Marianne's with us?" Connie asked, clutching her ragdoll.

"No, my dear. I will be at the farm." Suzie tucked her in tightly and smoothed her hair. "I need to live on the farm again and work with my father, but you can visit me and come and stay."

"But we need you here!"

"Who will look after us?" The girls chorused their laments, and Suzie felt a lump in her throat.

"I will miss you both so much, and I will always love you, but I need to go home. Your daddy will find another nice lady to look after you."

"But she might not know how to make crafts like you."

"Or be any fun."

"Or like us."

Now, both girls were sobbing, and Suzie was blinking back tears.

"You can teach her how to do crafts, how to sing our songs, and where to go for the best evening walks."

"But what if we don't like her?"

"Then you tell your father, and if he doesn't listen, you tell Auntie Marianne. She is extremely good at sorting things out."

"And we will run away to you," added Prue.

"Yes," agreed Suzie, "And I will march up here and put my hands on my hips, like this, and say, 'Now Miss Whatsyourname, you just listen to me. You are getting it all wrong with the lovely Mortimer girls. Prue likes blue ribbons in her hair, not orange-dotty ones. Connie must have honey mixed in with her morning milk, or she will turn green and be sick all over you. And don't you even know how to make a chain of paper dolls without

128

them falling apart? You should be ashamed of yourself. Whoever brought you up?"

The girls began to smile through their tears.

"I will march into the kitchen—'Date cake?'—this is totally unacceptable! The girls like chocolate chip biscuits after school. Here is the recipe, but add extra chocolate. And you had better be listening while we sing you our rainy-day song because I want it word-perfect by tomorrow."

"And what if she doesn't laugh like you?"

"Then I will frog-march her to a looking glass—'Miss Whatsyourname, just have a look in the mirror. What do you see? A long, straight face? Who wants to see that all day? Now, you just pick up those dreary ends of your mouth and make them go upwards. Keep them going up until they make your eyes twinkle. You stand here every day and practise until you are good at it. Then when you are good at smiling, we will see if we can teach you to laugh."

Before the girls could raise another objection, Suzie asked,

"What toys does Auntie Marianne have in her playroom?"

"She has a big rocking horse," they chorused.

"With a real horse-hair tail!"

"And lots of dollies."

"All with really pretty clothes you can take off and on."

"Even nappies."

"And the nursery nurse sometimes lets us play hospitals with them."

"She can even take one's arm off, and we will make it all better."

"And there is a proper little tea set we can use to give them drinks."

Suzie kissed them both goodnight.

"Chat away for a few more minutes if you want to, girls, and then it is time to settle down."

129

As she descended the stairs, she could still hear them discussing the delights of Auntie Marianne's house and garden. She smiled; they were going to be all right.

CHAPTER 26

It wasn't until she witnessed Elsie and Charlie's distraught reaction to the news that the magnitude of the forthcoming change hit Lydia. As he explained the situation to them after the evening meal, Matthew looked so sad that Lydia had left her end of the table, stood behind his chair, and wrapped her arms around his neck. She kissed his bald patch and squeezed his shoulders, but had nothing to say. The thought crossed her mind for the hundredth time: *was there another way?* Maybe she should go instead. Matthew drew his crying children to him and sat them one on each knee, just like in old times. Lydia was secretly amazed at the depth of their sadness. For so much of the past year, Matthew had been distant and grumpy. Sometimes, she felt she was carrying the family, and he was no more than a lodger. But now, she realised that, however he may have behaved, the bond the children had with him was firm and strong.

"I'll leave school and work!" Charlie exclaimed.

"And I can do more sewing!" volunteered Elsie.

Matthew shook his head slowly.

"This afternoon, I made a quick trip to Milford Train Station and visited the railway office. Just a few miles down the track, they are extending the line to link further towns to the London line. That is a big undertaking, and they need lots of men. If I present myself there next Monday morning, they will probably have a job for me."

"Will you be using explosives to clear the way?" Charlie asked excitedly. Lydia shuddered.

"There is a strange thing about work, Charlie. If you spend all day grafting, using all your muscles with a spade and shovel, out in all weathers, you don't get as well paid as people in warm offices, using just a pen and their brains. It doesn't seem fair, does it?"

Charlie agreed.

"Well, I've always liked those muscle sort of jobs. But now, I think I need to try one of the brain sort of jobs and, hopefully, get more money for you all."

"…And get home quicker," Elsie added.

"And get home quicker," Matthew agreed.

Lydia was relieved that her husband hadn't given Charlie a "now you are the man of the house" lecture. How any adult can thrust that sort of responsibility onto the slim shoulders of a little boy seemed ridiculous. And rather insulting to the grown woman of the house. They would all man up together.

The family's mood was heavy and depressing. Everyone moved as if carrying stones in their pockets. Monday! It was too close! Matthew did every job he had been putting off for the last few months. The squeaky door hinge got oil. The washing-line got a new rope, coal was ordered, and the chimney was swept. Lydia washed and mended all his clothes, darned his socks, and made him a kitbag. She bought him a tin cup, plate, and bowl, then sat and cried over them as she imagined him eating alone somewhere, miles away.

Lydia sat and cried for all the generations of women the world over who had packed the kitbags of their husbands and sons in far worse situations than the ones she faced. Husbands going to the battlefield, sons subscripted into the navy, or the man of the house facing incarceration in a debtor's prison. History books failed to mention the wives of intrepid explorers left at home to face the mundane daily challenges of domestic life and child-rearing alone while their husbands made a name for themselves. Even worse was the anguish of women made widows due to religious persecution. Lydia saluted every one of these women. Matthew was only going a few miles down the railway track, within the reach of the penny postal service. She had no excuse to feel sorry for herself. She admonished herself. This is when she needed to show her family what trust looks like. She needed to show by her attitude and actions that she had faith in her heavenly Father to look after the whole family. *Actions speak louder than words,* she often told the children. Now, she needed to demonstrate that. She pleaded for help from above—a real, childlike faith and a calm spirit were needed, not stoical endurance or a stiff English upper lip.

Friday morning found Lydia busy baking. She wanted Sunday tea to be extra special and for Matthew to take a few nibbles with his as a taste from home. He had gone to Milford to get his working boots repaired and, hopefully, visit Suzie and brief her on the situation. Lydia had wanted to go with him, but after much deliberation, they decided that the time would be better used if they divided forces. Now, Lydia felt they had made the wrong decision. Chores are important, and efficiency is the key to success, but time with loved ones is priceless and rarely regretted.

A knock at the front door interrupted her musings. It was unexpected, and she wondered if she had forgotten a dress-fitting arrangement.

"Mrs Lydia Griffen?" A bearded man with a rough straw hat and ruddy face filled her doorstep.

"That is me." The man lifted his hat and gave a sweeping bow.

"Then I have a delivery for you, madam." Looking beyond him, Lydia saw a delivery cart loaded with various cumbersome items.

The man whistled at a boy, who jumped onto the cart and started moving something heavy towards the tailgate. The big man went to help heave the shrouded object down to ground level.

"Are you sure you are at the right address, sir?" Lydia queried, "I don't think my husband has ordered any farm equipment recently."

The bearded man laughed, making his ruddy face even redder. "This machine is good for sewing but not sowing, ma'am." He appreciated his clever joke so much that he repeated it as he hauled the object up the garden path. "Ha, ha - good for sewing but not for sowing, ha, ha." The boy laughed politely, as if he realised that part of his role was to be an appreciative audience to his boss's wit.

Once in the dining room, the haulier paused for their eyes to adjust to the darkness. Then, with one deft movement and sense of drama any theatre actor would be proud of, he whipped off the dust cover to reveal a beautiful, shining Singer sewing machine on a polished wooden stand. Lydia's gasp of surprise encouraged the haulier to further dramatics.

"And all this is yours, Mrs Lydia Griffen!"

"Is there any explanation?" Lydia queried weakly.

Like a magician pulling a rabbit out of a hat, Mr Haulier pulled a letter from his breast pocket.

"All will be explained, madam."

And before she had time to offer him a drink or give him a tip, the flamboyant man disappeared out the door. Lydia sprang into action, found the money jar, and tipped a few coins into her hand. Grabbing some still-warm biscuits, she ran up the garden path after him. With much bowing and ingratiating smiles, the man pocketed the money and handed the biscuits to the lad. The haulier plonked himself onto the groaning cart seat, lifted his hat with a final flourish, shook the rains, and was gone.

Lydia returned indoors, sat at the table, and read the letter.

My dear Lydia

Please receive this sewing machine as a thank-you gift for the many kindnesses you bestowed on my late father. My dress-making business has been so busy recently that we have been able to employ another girl and invest in new sewing machines. The one I have sent you is a good and reliable workhorse. She has been cleaned, oiled, and repaired for your use. I know she will be well-loved and in good hands. I hope she will be useful to you. I enclose the original instruction manual, with a few added notes that may help as you begin.

With love and kind regards

Gwendoline

Lydia gazed at the beautiful machine. It was even powered by feet, so both hands were available to guide the material. Pulling up a kitchen chair to the machine, she sat down and cautiously pumped the treadle with her foot. The flywheel on the right started rotating, and the needle stabbed up and down. It was all so smooth and effortless. A wave of gratitude flooded over Lydia—gratitude to Gwendoline for her generosity, but above all, gratitude to her Heavenly Father. The timing of this gift was just so perfect. It was such a loving and practical token of His care and concern for her and her family.

The smell of burnt biscuits forcefully reminded Lydia of her original plan for the morning. Scurrying back to the kitchen, she rescued the tray of charred lumps from the stove—they were only fit for the hens now. By rushing through her chores, she made time to get acquainted with her new toy. Her scanty previous experience with sewing machines, plus the instruction manual, proved useful as she threaded up the machine and filled up the bobbin. Using old remnants of cloth, Lydia ran up her first seam. She gazed at it with awe and delight! The speed and neatness! So engrossed was she in her experimentation that Matthew's entrance went completely unnoticed.

"My, what have we here?" Lydia jumped and felt strangely guilty.

"A most kind and unexpected gift from Gwendoline," she hastily explained.

Matthew was smiling. She felt relieved. She was never quite sure how he viewed her money-making endeavours. He peered at the mechanics.

"It looks very useful."

"I think it will be revolutionary for my little business." As she said it, she realised she had never called her sewing a 'business' before.

"I am delighted for you." Matthew stood behind her and put his hands on her shoulders. "You deserve a bit of help, and I couldn't imagine a better gift."

Lydia turned her head and kissed his hand.

"I'll shave a little bit off the legs of this chair to make it exactly the right height," he continued.

Lydia smiled. Useful little acts like that were Matthew's language of love.

"How did Suzie take your news?" Lydia asked as she made him a cup of tea.

"Not too well," sighed Matthew as he sank into a chair. "I hadn't realised how much she looked forward to working alongside me."

"The two of you make a good team."

"Not too much can go wrong over the winter months. And she can always ask Caleb."

"Maybe that feels a bit awkward for her," wondered Lydia out loud.

"Awkward? What is awkward about asking a neighbour for advice?"

Lydia stared at her husband in amazement. She was about to open her mouth, but she stopped herself. Where would she begin trying to explain the discomfiture of a young, single woman, tentatively trying to make her own way in a man's world, admitting inadequacies to a young, highly suitable single man?

"I just thought it would be rather different from asking her dad for advice," Lydia answered lamely.

"She can always write to me," said Matthew, closing the conversation.

When she awoke on Monday morning, Matthew had already left the house. She vaguely remembered him brushing her cheek with a kiss, but she turned over and dozed on, thinking he was just getting up to light the stove. It wasn't until she was dressed and downstairs that she noticed his kit bag was gone. It was just like Matthew wanted to avoid a scene, especially if he would be its focus. She was annoyed at herself for falling back to sleep, not saying a proper goodbye, and not giving the children an opportunity to do so. But Matthew had done it his way and done it successfully, which was the important thing.

Lydia had little time to mope. The extra chores and a dress-fitting that afternoon banished any idea of indulging in self-pity.

CHAPTER 27

Suzie looked around her little bedroom and sighed with satisfaction. This is where she belonged. Tonight, she would be snuggled up next to Elsie, just like old times. All the smart town outfits she wore, like dressing-up costumes, were left behind in the wardrobe at the Mortimers. She had purchased them with a dress allowance that came with the role, and she could not decide if they belonged to her or Mr Mortimer. So, not wanting to be indebted to him in any way, shape, or form, she left them there, like discarded props at the end of a play. Suzie was no longer a townie. Now, she was a farm labourer. She relished the thought of donning her scruffy, practical frocks and getting stuck in.

That morning, she had seen the excited girls off in the White's carriage for their holiday with Auntie Marianne. After her last cup of tea with Molly, she had hoped to make a quiet, unnoticed exit, but as she was creeping down the stairs with her bags, Mr Mortimer had emerged from his study and, with exaggerated gallantry, opened the front door for her.

"Goodbye, Suzanna." She shook his cold, outstretched hand. "And I hope you don't regret your foolish decision, as spinsterhood as a peasant farmer loses its appeal."

"Thank you, Sir." Suzie smiled at him as she descended the steps to the pavement. Then to the now-shut door, "Please do not worry yourself on my behalf."

Suzie had feared that the first evening at home without her father would feel flat and empty, but Elsie had been hatching a plan and waiting for Suzie's help to execute it.

"Mama needs a proper place to do her sewing and dress fitting," she explained animatedly. "We too often come home from school and barge into a customer's conversation with her. Also, we don't need a dining room at the moment. Pa isn't here, and the only visitor we have is Caleb, who, at his house, eats in his kitchen with the dog by his side."

She had the family's full attention.

"So, I propose that we eat all our meals at the kitchen table, and sit by the kitchen stove in the evenings, and turn the dining room into Mama's workroom cum fitting room. She can use the table for cutting out fabric. The sewing machine can go near the window for good lighting for her eyes. We could even hang a curtain in one corner for a changing room for the customer."

"What would your father think?" Lydia asked cautiously.

"He would think it was economical to live in the kitchen. The dining room stove would only need lighting when you are working there. We will save ourselves a lot of log splitting and chopping. And it is cosy having evenings at the kitchen stove."

Suzie had never seen little Elsie look so enthusiastic and persuasive.

"I think it is a good idea," she agreed. Elsie beamed.

"Mama will have her very own, proper shop!" Charlie exclaimed, and they all laughed.

"Let's get going," Lydia suggested. And so they did!

The kitchen looked snug and a bit crowded, with the table pushed into a corner and the everyday armchairs placed near the stove. Lydia found a colourful rag rug –

"Once the cooking and daily chores are done, I can put this down, pull around the chairs, and we can settle into our evenings," she explained.

After the autumnal sun had set, they sat down together in their newly configured living quarters and enjoyed the cramped cosiness of the arrangement. Lydia knitted, Elsie sewed, but Suzie and Charlie just chatted. Everyone wondered aloud what Papa was doing right now and silently prayed for his safety. Charlie had tall stories of unruly pupils, and then Suzie told them about her last day at the Mortimers.

"Of course, Morose Mortimer had to have the last word just as I was leaving…"

"Stop!" interrupted Charlie, standing up. "Act it out, Suzie, using funny voices like you used to be good at."

Suzie laughed at him, "Okay, Charlie. You pretend to be me. Be carrying heavy bags. The sitting room door can be his front door."

Staggering exaggeratedly under the weight of imaginary bags, Charlie approached her. Suzie held out a limp hand, smirked a false smile, and said, in a deep, smarmy voice, "And I hope you don't regret your foolish decision as spinsterhood as a peasant farmer loses its appeal."

Everyone laughed, and Charlie wanted to repeat the scene with even more amateur dramatics. But just as they were finishing the act, the back door opened, and Caleb walked in. None had heard his quiet knock. Suzie, flustered and feeling foolish, sat down quickly. Why did the man always spring himself upon them so unexpectedly?

"Come on, Suzie. Show Caleb our acting," pestered Charlie. "He likes funny voices."

"No!" Suzie glared warningly at him.

"Oh, go on," persisted her annoying brother, unperturbed by her stare. "She is really good at acting, you know, Caleb."

"I bet she is, but maybe not now," Caleb answered tactfully.

Getting up almost as quickly as she had sat down, Suzie grabbed the teapot and asked, "Anyone for a cuppa?"

Caleb wasn't allowed to drink his tea before an excited Elsie had shown him the new sewing room. Grabbing his hand, she dragged him off and could be heard enthusiastically explaining the virtues of the new arrangement. Suzie felt a pang of jealousy at Elsie's ease with their neighbour.

When they had returned and were sipping their evening drinks, the conversation flowed naturally, meandering all over the place. This, Suzie decided, is what she had missed during the long, lonely evenings at the Mortimer's.

"Are you going to get straight stuck into farming tomorrow, Suzie?" Caleb asked, "Or will you ease yourself in gently?"

"I think I need to go in headlong," Suzie replied. "Apple picking is almost upon us. After doing the daily care of the livestock, I thought I might get the wicker picking baskets and bushel boxes down from the stable attic and give them a good brush down, ready for apple-ing."

She hoped she sounded organised and efficient.

Caleb nodded. "Sounds like a good idea. This apple-ing is all new to me. I'd never even seen an orchard up close until I came down south. I need to order a stencil to put my name on all of Mr Baillie's old bushel boxes. I found stacks of them in his old diary and need to get them ready for apples, too."

"If you help me get mine out the loft, I'll help you get yours out the old diary," suggested Suzie.

"Excellent!" agreed Caleb, getting to his feet. "And now, I need to shut in the hens, then hit the sack." Ruffing up Charlie's hair, he continued, "Come on, lad, you can shut in your hens for your big sister, can't you?" And instead of moaning about it, as he would if Suzie had asked, Charlie happily scampered after Caleb and did as he was bidden.

The next few days were tiring but productive. The wicker apple baskets and bushel boxes were dragged out of their cobwebby storage, brushed off and repaired, and ladders for the pickers were also gathered from the various places they were last used. She and Caleb worked together, but Suzie wished their rapport could be less stilted. He was doing his best—he was industrious and businesslike in a cheerful manner that was pleasing and positive. He was neither too taciturn nor chatty. He was gentlemanly without being patronising. Suzie longed for the easy relationship Elsie had with him. She wondered what he really thought of her—deep down, did he really approve of a woman trying to do a man's job? Men, especially chapel men, could be very traditional and old-fashioned in their views. Was she working hard enough and pulling her weight, or did he think he was doing more than his fair share? He gave her no reason to suspect that, but he was a kind and polite man, so he would be unwilling to voice these opinions. His conversation could be witty and lively. Did he find her responses too mundane and predictable? These questions stifled her playfulness and made her feel even more bored. But why, she asked herself, should she care anyway? He was just a neighbour and fellow worker, wasn't he? He was, but she had to admit that he was also a thoroughly decent and pleasant lad, too.

On Sunday, Suzie was pleased to be back in her family's pew, under the gallery, at the rear of the chapel. Mr Mortimer cut a solitary figure as he sat, ramrod straight in his almost-empty pew. Looking at him with his impeccably creamed hair, heavily starched collar, and pristine pin-striped suit, Suzie felt nothing but relief. Glancing to her right, Suzie could see Caleb bent forward, deep in prayer. His blond hair looked as if it had been lain on wrongly all night and had refused to be tamed by a comb or water. His best collar showed signs of age and probably would benefit from a turn. His worshipful demeanour was a rebuke to Suzie's wandering thoughts, and she attempted to fix her mind on higher things.

The pastor preached warmly and winsomely from Psalm 100. Like the psalmist, he not only urged the people to praise the Lord but also gave them compelling reasons for doing so. He explained what a blessing it was to have our Lord as our God—not some self-obsessed and vindictive heathen god, but a good God, abundant in mercy and truth. He quoted Spurgeon in saying, *"Our happy God should be worshipped by a happy people; a cheerful spirit is in keeping with His nature, His acts, and the gratitude which we should cherish for His mercies."* It had never entered Suzie's head that the God of the Bible—her God—was a happy God, but the thought thrilled her. In this short psalm, all the mentions of joy, gladness, singing, thanksgiving, and praise emphasise the idea of a good God who gives with lavish enjoyment and who lovingly requires our joyful, wholehearted trust and confidence.

As the minister spoke of the Lord skilfully and tenderly shepherding the sheep of His pasture, Suzie's thoughts ran through recent events in her life. In her darkest times, the Lord had protected her and placed just the right people in her path. He had gradually opened her eyes to the simplicity of the way of salvation. He had shown her the willingness of the Lord Jesus to save and His trustworthiness in keeping His promises. He had warmed her cold, doubting heart with a glow of love for Him. All this had been done tenderly, gently, and irresistibly.

When the minister came to the last verse and spoke of the Lord's truth enduring to all generations, she glanced at the empty place where her father used to sit. A stab of sadness was mixed with a surge of gratitude that the Lord's mercy and goodness were everlasting and encompassed loved ones near and far for time and for eternity.

The service ended with the singing of "All people that on earth do dwell", the metrical version of the psalm, sung to the tune of Old Hundreth, and it was indeed "seemly so to do." Glancing over at Caleb, Suzie saw him singing heartily without needing the hymnbook. *I expect he also knows it in Gaelic*, she thought, and wondered if singing a psalm made him feel a little homesick for Scotland and his family.

"I wonder if Papa is feeling homesick," voiced Charlie, tucking into his mutton stew.

Until that moment, the atmosphere had been fairly bright. Lydia had enjoyed the service as much as Suzie and had hummed Old Hundreth as she served the meal. Suzie harmonised with the alto as she laid the table. At Charlie's remark, Elsie burst into tears and fled upstairs.

"That wasn't very clever," snapped Suzie to her brother.

"I was just wondering. How was I to know she would be a crybaby about it?" replied Charlie through a mouth full of food.

"Charlie! Manners!" Lydia chided semi-automatically before bolting upstairs to comfort and retrieve Elsie. Once everyone was together again and peace reigned, Lydia tried to reassure her children.

"It is a blessing that your father has a day of rest, like us today. It must be tiring to follow the railway line looking for work. I expect he has found a little chapel in Sussex to attend. I hope and trust that some kind folks from the congregation have invited him in for a nice, warm meal. It is a mercy we can commit his welfare to the Lord, isn't it?"

They all nodded in sombre agreement.

"I thought Caleb was coming to dinner," Elsie said, breaking the long silence.

"He had been invited elsewhere," Lydia replied. "I spoke to him yesterday. He will probably come here for tea, though."

Charlie perked up. "He gets a lot of invitations to Sunday dinner." He explained to Suzie, "Pa says especially from families with single daughters."

"Charlie!" Lydia admonished him again.

"It's true, though, isn't it?" Charlie insisted indignantly.

"Some things that are true are best left unsaid," his mother explained.

"I don't see why," protested Charlie. "He gets a lot of free dinners 'cos he is single and…"

"Just be quiet for once, will you!?" barked Suzie, feeling inordinately annoyed.

That evening, the minister preached a lovely sermon about the little Israelitish maid of Naaman's wife in 2 Kings chapter 5. He dramatically imagined her being kidnapped from her loving family and transported to a foreign land with a foreign language and foreign gods. Suzie could see he had the attention of all the children as he explained her awful plight. Yet he went on to explain that despite all her trauma, she was not bitter or vindictive but remained trusting in the Lord and caring towards others. He drew out lessons for his hearers, saying that however small and insignificant they might feel, their God is almighty and they should speak up, even just a few words for Him. He also told his congregation that holding a grudge was never justified. If a little girl could feel sympathy for an army general who had been responsible for masterminding the slaughter and plunder of her people, we have no excuse to nurse grievances. Suzie felt rebuked, and looking at the ramrod back and the shiny bald patch of Mr Mortimer, she prayed for help. She thought further back to the awful Mr Briggs. She didn't even want to forgive him, not for what he had done to her or what he was doing—hoodwinking the poor old dowager. Could you forgive someone yet still hope they get their comeuppance? She prayed for a right and clean heart in all her thinking processes.

After the service, Caleb came to tea, and it was just as well that he did, as the whole family were feeling a bit heartsick for Papa. The busyness of the week masked his absence, but the quiet routine of Sunday seemed to highlight it. His place had been vacant at the dinner table and in their pew. They had missed his melodious bass voice during the hymns, him reading articles from The Little Gleaner magazine to them after dinner, and all the other insignificant things they had barely noticed before that now left painful gaps.

"Pastor was in fine form today," commented Caleb as he tucked into a cheese sandwich.

"Yes," agreed Lydia, "I particularly enjoyed this morning about the Lord's goodness."

"His quote from Spurgeon particularly struck me, about our God being a happy God," Suzie added.

"Me too! I've never heard it put like that before and have been toying with the idea ever since." Caleb looked animatedly at her. "I'm not sure the Bible ever calls God happy, but it often says He rejoices."

"Jesus said to His disciples, 'These things have I spoken unto you, that my joy might remain in you and that your joy might be full,'" quoted Suzie.

"Happiness and blessedness in the Bible are always linked to holiness," Lydia added.

"Yes," agreed Caleb thoughtfully, "Heaven is God's home, as in 'In my Father's house are many mansions', and is the place of supreme happiness and holiness because that is His character."

They munched in contented silence as they mused on the subject. Suzie was so thankful to have like-minded people to digest the sermon with. This was a blessing that neither the servant's hall at the

Manor nor the Mortimer's dining room had afforded her. She looked at her mother, her weathered face beautified by gentleness, love, and wisdom, and felt a surge of affection. She looked at Caleb and experienced an almost identical emotion. Immediately, she corrected herself: *remember all his Sunday dinner invitations.* She threw all her attention into making a fresh pot of tea.

By the time the meal had ended, it was almost too dark for a walk, but Lydia shooed the others out the door.

"I insist you leave me to do the washing up. I'll get a bit of time to myself. You get some fresh air. Tish and Charlie need a bit of exercise."

None could argue with that.

For the first half of the walk, Elsie and Charlie vied for Caleb's attention. Suzie was happy to hang back and listen with amusement. On the return journey, Charlie asked,

"Where did you have dinner today, then, Caleb?"

Suzie's ears pricked up.

"Oh, I went to old Mr and Mrs Tailor's again. They are quite lonely now that their children have all flown the nest. And they knew my father."

"How lovely!" exclaimed Suzie, with more enthusiasm than the facts deserved.

"Yes, it was," agreed Caleb, falling back to walk alongside her. "They are such a dear, godly couple."

"Yes, they are. Mr Tailor was my Sunday school teacher at one time."

"They both spoke very highly of you, Suzie."

"Me?" Suzie gasped. Why were they talking about her? "I don't think I was a particularly good pupil for him."

"They said how kind you were to Mr Baillie."

"Oh, that was a while ago. Ma was the kindest." She quickly changed the conversation. "It must be nice chatting with people who know your pa."

"Yes, it really is. It also makes me feel a wee bit homesick."

"You are from a big, close family, aren't you?"

Lying in bed later that evening, Caleb felt silly that he had chatted in such great detail about his family and their croft. The poor girl was probably bored and bewildered by so many names: who was married to whom, who had which children, and all their strange Gaelic-sounding names. Was she really interested in the landscape, the concept of hefting, and him introducing cattle to their valley, or was she just being extremely kind to him? Or maybe just polite. But without a doubt, she was an excellent listener and asked intelligent questions, and somehow, maybe partly due to the twilight, he had been turned into a chatterbox. He almost heard his brothers mocking him for becoming such an old *blellum*.

CHAPTER 28

Suzie stared in dismay at the assembled team of apple pickers. She and Caleb had spent the previous week doing further preparations for the apple harvest and got on like a house on fire. They had brished under all the apple trees- cutting down all the stinging nettles and thistles with short scythes. Using her father's contacts, they had made a business arrangement with a Covent Garden Market stall holder to sell their fruit. . They had repaired and oiled the smallest flat-bed waggon for carting the bushel boxes to Milton train station. They both felt excitement and pride at the thought of having their produce sold in the capital. Suzie tried to feel like a fully-fledged businesswoman but couldn't get beyond the feeling of a school girl pretending.

Last week, Caleb had assured her that enough locals had expressed an interest in apple-picking to fulfil their daily quota with the stall holder. In her mind's eye, Suzie remembered the motley crew of older villagers who turned up for seasonal work hoping to put away a bit of savings for the winter months. Within the assembled group today were some of those stalwarts, but alongside them was an alarming gaggle of giggling young women. Suzie immediately recognised them as Miltonites. They had been contemporaries of her at the village school. They had rich parents, so they did not have to curtail their education early and enter service, like her Brookfield friends. They were some of the sniggering bunch that despised the villagechildren. How odd that they were here! Suzie felt her confidence ebb away. The old-timers were dressed like Suzie in comfortable, scruffy clothes, enwrapped in sack aprons with huge pockets for collecting apples when on a ladder. The newbie pickers looked like they were in a fashion parade, with tight corsets and fancy frocks.

"Well, here we are, Mr Farmer, bright and early, ready to be good little farmeresses," flirted the ringleader.

The girls laughed and joked as they collected their picking baskets. Suzie looked on nervously. She and Caleb had agreed that, before commencing picking, a short lecture should be given to one and all, explaining the quality of apples and picking the London market expected. Caleb, being new to apple-ing, suggested Suzie do the lecture. Suzie, imagining she would be addressing the normal bunch of experienced pickers, had agreed.

Climbing up on the flat-bedded waggon so all could hear her, Suzie experienced stage fright. Caleb caught her eye and seemed to understand. He vaulted up onto the waggon next to her, "I'll get their attention and introduce you."

"Welcome to you all. Thank you for coming to help Miss Griffen and me bring in the apple harvest." A wolf whistle and clapping could be heard from the gaggle. "Each afternoon, the day's pick will be shipped up to London to Covent Garden Market" (another wolf whistle). "Of course, our picking must be of a high standard. If we are deemed to fall below the requirements in how we handle the apples, the quality of the apples we send, or the quantity, our contract may be terminated. Therefore, Miss Griffen will explain to you all about the quality of picking we are asking for. Thank you." All this was delivered in a commanding and sonorous voice.

Suzie opened her mouth and squeaked, "I have a selection of apples here to illustrate what should be discarded. The first one is obvious—it is party rotten. Gently throw such apples on the floor under the tree. The next..." Suzie's mouth was dry, and her voice was grating. She felt apologetic to the seasoned pickers, who knew more than she did and felt as if the fancy girls had already despised her. With steely determination, she went on to describe how to pick an apple without leaving finger marks by using the palm of your hand. She demonstrated how to gently tip apples from the picking baskets to the bushel boxes. Finally, she explained how the pickers would be paid per bushel boxs and how she and Caleb would walk around the orchard, inspecting each picker's boxes for quality.

Suzie was relieved to have finished; she had gabbled it through far too fast.

"Well done, lass," said old Mr Wilmore, who had picked apples for her grandfather. Suzie smiled gratefully at him.

Suzie hardly saw Caleb for the rest of the morning. They were busy showing each picker which row to start on, distributing buckets and ladders, and then transporting bushel boxes down the rows with the horse and cart. The girls had all flocked to Caleb and the villagers to Suzie, and her team were quickly filling their boxes with quality produce. From the other side of the orchard wafted snippets of high-spirited chatter and laughter. Suzie felt rather dull and boring. The villagers were by no means silent or sullen, but their discussion was more about the weather, the crop compared with previous years, and reminiscing about people they used to pick who were no longer with them. Suzie enjoyed their chat and would have liked to hide away with them all day, but she was concerned about the amateur group on the other end. Once she was satisfied they had enough empty bins to keep them going, Suzie made her way over to Caleb.

He strolled to meet her, grinning with satisfaction.

"I've given them all a row, and I think they are making good progress."

"Good," Suzie replied cautiously, "but I will reserve judgement until I have inspected their bushel boxes."

"I'll join you and learn."

With a show of confidence she did not possess, Suzie approached the first picker and her bushel.

"Good morning, Miss...?"

"Miss Marchant, but call me Maddie."

"Maddie, I'll just have a look through your bushel and see how you are doing."

"Go ahead."

Suzie carefully dove into the bushel. She picked out one or two cracked apples and showed them to Maddie, who nodded.

"Sorry," apologised Suzie, "but we have to be fussy because the London market is."

Suzie moved slowly through the rows.

"Sorry, I can see finger marks here. They are only faint today, but tomorrow in London, they will be very obvious bruises."

"Sorry, you shouldn't have moved on to the next tree. There are lots more here. You need to use your ladder for the top ones."

Suzie knew she was apologising too much. She knew she looked awfully picky, but this was their biggest source of income and their reputation as producers.

"Hey, catch this, Miss Griffen," sang out a picker, tossing an apple to her. The rotten apple squelched into her hand as she caught it.

A roar of mirth erupted from the group.

Suzie whipped her hands on the grass and moved on.

Caleb said, "That wasn't funny," but not loudly enough.

As the September sun became hotter and the thick dew evaporated off the trees and grass, Lydia came from the house bearing a large jug of lemonade. Most people received it gratefully; nothing was as refreshing as lemonade on a hot day, and the older villagers realised the expense of lemons and the generosity of offering such a delicious treat.

The girls drank it down enthusiastically, but Suzie heard some cutting remarks about "quaint rustic practices" and "the old peasant farmer's wife." She wanted to either cry or scream. Whatever had possessed Caleb to invite these females into his orchard? The day dragged on. At lunchtime, she went indoors, but not before she had seen various girls eagerly offering Caleb a share of their packed lunch.

Ma and Elsie were busy jamming baskets of blackberries, slows, and damsons from the hedgerows. The kitchen smelt delicious, the sun was shining, the sky was blue, and they were surrounded by an abundance. Suzie knew she should be happy, but she felt miserable. She dreaded another inspection round this afternoon, but knew it was vitally important. She would be disappointed in Caleb if he didn't have it in him to ensure a high standard.

After checking on the old handers, she went back to the girls. Caleb was busy looking through bushels.

"Who picked these?" he asked. "This one is bruised."

"Ahh, Caleb, aren't you a tough man on an inexperienced girl?" the picker moaned.

"We have to be."

"He's a man who knows what he wants," teased another girl.

Caleb moved on.

Soon, it was time to collect all the bushel boxes on the waggon. Caleb wrote down how many bushels each had picked.

"Shall we go then?" he asked Suzie as he climbed onto the waggon and took the reins.

Suzie shook her head, "I think I should stay here."

"But we agreed to go to the train station together. These bushels all need unloading at the other end."

"I hadn't anticipated the inexperience of your work team," Suzie replied icily before turning her back to him and walking off.

Caleb trundled gloomily to Milford. He had been looking forward to a daily trip with Suzie. He was perplexed at her chilliness. Seeing her in the orchard earlier today, clearly knowledgeable about her trade, with her hair all unruly, her sleeves rolled up, and looking so businesslike in that huge apron, he'd longed to brush the mud off her cheek. But that 'Do not disturb' look she flashed just now startled him. The group of lasses this morning had taken him by surprise. The only one he recognised was Maddie. Her grandmother, Mrs Ayres, went to Brookfield's chapel and had invited him to Sunday dinner a few times. Maddie had always been there, "helping to entertain him," as her grandmother put it. The expression had rather annoyed Caleb, as if he were a demanding little boy who needed someone to keep him occupied. The grandmother's conversation was far more interesting than the granddaughter's, as she had lots of local historical knowledge to impart. Maddie, on the other hand, always seemed to be attempting wit, often at other people's expense, and failing. When Mrs Ayres mentioned last week that she knew a few people interested in apple picking, Caleb hadn't imagined it would be Maddie.

CHAPTER 29

"Mrs Ayres!" Lydia angrily exclaimed, "That woman is the biggest busybody and the most incurable matchmaker in the village."

"What has she got to do with our new pickers?" Suzie asked as she was setting the table.

"Well, I saw her last week in the bakery, and she was asking about the farm (you know how she pries) and especially about our young neighbour. She prattled on about all sorts of things, including bemoaning the fact that her granddaughter, Maddie, was on the shelf."

"On the shelf? She can't be more than nineteen!"

"Also bemoaning that Maddie lives a vacuous life due to her parents' wealth."

"I didn't know Mrs Ayres led the most industrious life herself," commented Suzie.

"Oh, she puts her finger in most of the charitable pies in the locality."

Lydia was feeling rather out of sorts. She always felt that she should like jam making—picking an abundance of ripe fruits and berries in the beautiful sun-kissed countryside, filling the larder with colourful rows of bounty for her family to eat during the barren winter months, and the secret satisfaction of knowing one's recipes are the best in the village. But she did not like it. Picking fruit was pleasurable, but that is where her pleasure ended. The endless stoning of plums and damsons, the constant stoking of the stove on warm days, the sugary stickiness that mixed with sweat as she stirred the bubbling saucepans and boiled water to clean the jars, and the feeling of missing out as the last warmth of the summer's sun beamed enticingly through the kitchen window. Then came the inevitable disappointment of far fewer jars of jam than anticipated, not to mention the shocking price of sugar. Jam making and pickling seemed to demand her undivided attention and energy, to the exclusion of all other household chores, much like a colicky baby might. Then, the housewifely guilt of neglecting the home and family reared its ugly and all-too-familiar head.

This year, her guilt was amplified threefold. She wished she'd offered more support to Suzie in the orchard. She scolded herself for keeping Elsie off school to help, and she imagined the unfinished frocks in the dining room frowning at her negligence.

The uncertainty of her husband's whereabouts and situation was also troubling her. She scolded herself about that, too. The way she fretted and feared for his safety was so unbefitting for a person who professed to believe in a Heavenly Father's care. One minute she was committing her husband into the Lord's hands; the next, she was more or less suggesting to the all-wise God how He could order events best. No sooner had she repented of such audacity than she found herself doing it again.

But as she thought about it all, she became all muddled up. The Lord encourages us to pray—"In everything by prayer and supplication with thanksgiving, let your requests be made known unto God." She was not trying to give God good ideas; she was just supplicating and requesting. And after each request, she submitted herself to His wise providence by saying, "Thy will be done." As she mused upon prayer and how it interacts with God's eternal purposes, she realised afresh that the wisest theologians are only in the infant class of learning about Him. She also wondered if she let 'the accuser of the saints' have too much say in her conscience. The devil condemns and castigates, but "like as a father pitieth his children, so the Lord pitieth them that fear him. For He knoweth our frame; He remembereth that we are dust."

Suzie ate her dinner in silence. She was exhausted from her day of managing the pickers, and her limbs longed for bed. But that wasn't the main cause of her gloom. Just as she was beginning to realise Caleb's sterling qualities, an awful realisation dawned on her, sparked by Mabel's arrival and her Ma's conversation at the baker's. Caleb was ambitious. He had left his entire clan in Scotland to branch out alone. She knew he wouldn't settle for being a tenant farmer forever; he had told her as much last week. What a young, aspiring bachelor farmer needed most was money. The easiest way to acquire money was to marry into it. He may be a principled Christian (of that she had no doubt), but thinking of some of her own peers in the village, love made fools of them. Caleb could easily convince himself that he was acting prudently by avoiding marrying into a peasant family (as they were called today) and seeking financial security (which farming can never offer). Mabel, or any of the Milford bunch, would also look far more decorative on his arm than she ever could. She was surprised at how deeply this hurt.

Suzie felt like moping about all evening, but she looked at her mother and saw the same exhaustion mirrored back. It galvanised her into action.

"Righty ho, Elsie, you and I should wash and dry up. Charlie, you need to fill the log baskets, and then we need to do the outside chores before the light fades. Ma, you go and have a little lie-down. We insist."

Lydia did not have a little lie down; instead, she went to her new sewing room and hemmed a dress. That, she felt, was more beneficial. She felt she had accomplished something, and hopefully, she would sleep better for not having an evening nap.

The following day dawned chilly and misty. The dew-drenched apple trees soon soaked the pickers. Suzie was surprised and disappointed to see the Milton ladies back and ready for action. Social life in the town must be at a very low ebb, she thought. The girls were full of self-congratulations for turning up again and flirtatiously fished for compliments from Caleb. They all but ignored Suzie.

As the hot sun broke through and evaporated the mist, the light-hearted atmosphere of the girls also began to vaporise.

Suzie, once again, had to point out some finger marks, cracked apples, and bruises. One of the girls caught her lace-trimmed sleeve on a branch, and it ripped. Maddie was stung by a wasp and cried. All the girls stopped working to console her and dramatised at each wasp they sighted. Then, in the distance, there was a rumble of thunder. Enough was enough! Leaving their half-filled baskets and almost empty bushels, the girls fled back to the civilisation of Milford before they got soaked.

The rain never came, but the girls never returned. Suzie's mood lightened—now, the normal, comradery atmosphere of apple picking pervaded the orchard. The villagers sang, chatted, and joked. They all sat together at lunchtime and reminisced. In the afternoon, they enjoyed Ma's tangy lemonade. She was looking more relaxed and lingered longer in the congenial company.

At about mid-afternoon, Lydia came bounding up to Suzie. "Look, I have a letter from your father!" she called, beaming at her.

Suzie rubbed her grubby hands on her apron and grabbed the letter.

My dear Lydia and children,

I am very thankful to have suitable employment. I ventured further along the rail track each day, seeking work, but most of the posts were filled. Money was getting very tight. I heard say that the railway company was tunnelling near Sharpthorne, so made my way to the site.

How I received my post was most remarkable—for two days, I laboured as a member of the construction crew. The work was hard and dangerous. I was in lodgings at an inn, but the company was raucous, and sleeping was difficult. On Wednesday evening, wishing to set my mind on higher things, I attended a prayer meeting at a small chapel in the village. I felt such unity with the dear folks there. After many prayers had been offered, I joined in and prayed earnestly for the safety of all the men working on the new tunnel (it weighs heavily on me).

After the service, a smartly dressed man approached me. He turns out to be the head of the payroll team for the Sharpthorne Tunnel project. He had been looking for an honest man to help him with clerical work in the office, and he offered me the job there and then. I most thankfully accepted and am enjoying higher wages and more congenial work and company.

As I was walking back to the inn, an old lady from the congregation also stopped me. She and her husband were seeking a lodger. Once again, I had reason to thank the Lord for His kind provision.

I hope the apple picking is going well. Don't leave the baskets out overnight.

With much love to you all,

Matthew Griffen

Suzie hugged her mother with joy.

"How wonderful!" she exclaimed.

"So many prayers answered," agreed Lydia, looking years younger than yesterday.

From the high foliage of a tree, Caleb called out, asking for the news.

"Matthew'sa got a job. He is a clerical assistant for the railway line, and he has good lodgings," sang out Lydia.

Caleb's grinning face appeared through the leaves. "Oh, I am so glad."

Everyone enjoyed the afternoon. Elsie baked apple turnovers for everyone, and the beautiful late summer weather continued without a cloud in the sky. Caleb and Suzie no longer had to spend most of their time inspecting other people's picking so they could join in. The day's pick was very satisfactory in quality and quantity. When Caleb asked her to accompany him to Milton Station with the bushels this time, Suzie agreed. Trundling along the lane, perched next to him on the bench, with the cart full of their produce behind, Suzie felt her optimism return.

But after a general chit-chat (which seemed easier when you are both looking straight ahead and not requiring eye contact), Suzie voiced the question for which she felt Caleb owed her an answer.

"Why did you invite Maddie and the other girls apple picking?"

"Invite them!?" Caleb sounded shocked. "Do you think I would invite them? They just turned up."

"But you said you had a few volunteers for apple picking, so I assume you knew they were coming."

"No, I didn't know. Mrs Ayres told me last week that she had told people about the apple picking, and several said they would be coming. I was in a hurry; I didn't ask for names, and she didn't give any."

"Oh, I see," said Suzie, and added, trying to sound light, "So they aren't a bunch you fraternise with regularly?"

"Fraternise?" Caleb sounded hurt. "Do you think I am the sort of lad to fraternise with silly lasses like them?"

"No, I suppose not."

"Good!" replied Caleb, still slightly irritated. "No more than you fraternising with Mr Mortimer."

"What has Mr Mortimer got to do with it?"

There was a long, uncomfortable pause.

"I suppose I am just saying that we shouldn't judge each other by the people who are forced upon us from time to time."

"Hmm," agreed Suzie, relieved they were turning onto Station Road and would soon be too busy unloading to continue the conversation.

The tension in the air had gone by the time they were on their return journey. Suzie, fascinated by the history of the Highlands and the plight of the poor crofters, asked more about the Scottish estate of the D'Egertons. Caleb's family highly regarded Lady Isabel, and Suzie explained how fond she became of the old lady during their walks in London. Some of the stories she recounted to Suzie on those walks linked directly to the Baker family.

"What made you leave your beloved strath to come to Kent?" Suzie asked, puzzled by how anyone could pull themselves away from such beauty and family history.

"Being the youngest brother, I guess there wasn't really room for me to make a mark there." Caleb gazed at the road ahead.

"It must have been a big wrench to leave all your kith and kin behind."

"Something happened that made me need to get out."

Suzie felt she couldn't pry any further, so she remained silent.

"I may as well tell you, Suzie. I think you will understand. I was engaged to a lovely lass called Annella. She was a maid for the minister in the local congregation. During the winter before our wedding, when our strath was cut off from everyone, I was busy making the finishing touches to our little house and dreaming of her making quilts and things for it too. All the while, a student of divinity who was lodging with the minister was worming his way into Annella's affections by teaching her how to read. The long and short of it is that she married him and not me."

"Oh, Caleb! I am sorry; that must have hurt!" Suzie's sympathy melted Caleb.

"Yes, it did!" Caleb agreed ruefully, "But it also hurt my pride. I felt all my brothers would deride and pity me."

"No one would!" Suzie contradicted warmly.

"I see that now."

"Do you regret coming South and leaving them all?"

"No, not at all. I needed time to get over Annella. I cared for her deeply. I've recovered and had the opportunity to try different sorts of farming enterprises. I really appreciate the preaching here in Brookfield. I've met some lovely people—especially a certain Griffen family—who have all been exceptionally kind. So no, no regrets."

"That's good."

"And you, Suzie? Has your heart ever been broken?" Caleb teased.

Suzie flushed with embarrassment. If anyone were going to break it, it would be him.

"Oh!" she joked, "I am struggling to recover from the pain of wrenching myself away from Mr Melancholy Mortimer."

"No one else?"

"Where would I find time for such liaisons?"

"I know the feeling."

They jogged along, both deep in their own thoughts. Just as they were turning into the farmyard, Caleb broke the silence.

"By the way, Suzie, I haven't told anyone else about Annella. Please keep it to yourself."

Suzie looked at him intensely.

"Of course I will. But, Caleb, you shouldn't be ashamed of that episode in your life. You were not to blame. The hurt that you felt does you credit."

"How so?"

Suzie blushed. "It shows how deeply you can love."

And with that, she sprang off the cart and headed home.

Lydia only felt the tiniest bit guilty about inviting Caleb to the evening meal. When they were busy on the farm, she often felt it was a pity that he had to go and cook for himself, especially when it was easy for her to increase her meal preparations by one portion. But Matthew had always disagreed: "He didn't come down south to be molly-coddled by a mother figure. Let him be the self-sufficient bachelor he wants to be." But having read Matthew's letter today and being so thankful to the old woman hosting her husband, she ignored his opinion and issued the invitation. It was readily accepted.

"Put out an extra place setting, Suzie. Caleb is coming," she instructed.

"Oh!" Suzie sounded surprised. "He didn't mention that just now. Are we celebrating Pa's letter?"

"Yes, I suppose so, and just being supportive of our business partner."

"Good idea!" Suzie agreed warmly.

As soon as Caleb had stabled and fed Chestnut, the mare, he spruced himself up and made his way to the Griffen's cottage.

Lydia welcomed him, "Come on in, Caleb."

"It is very kind of you to do this, Lydia," he said, taking his seat at the table.

He turned to Suzie, "Sorry, I forgot to mention that I had been invited to fraternise here tonight."

"Fraternise!?" exclaimed Lydia. "What a strange way of..." Her sentence trailed off when she saw the two of them exchange a knowing look and smile. She even suspected Caleb had winked. She was glad.

CHAPTER 30

Everyone gazed in awe and admiration at the elegant London bank cheque. Matthew had, of course, received many such cheques over the years, but they were always rapidly pocketed and banked before curious eyes could read the numbers. But this year, they all shared the satisfaction of seeing the princely amount and the sense of security. John's fees and the rent could be paid. The cheque was payable to Mr M Griffen. Charlie thought they should cut it in half so Mr C Baker could have his share, but Lydia explained that she would bank the cheque the next day and transfer half into Caleb's account. The first thing she did the next morning was hitch up the mare and ride into Milford. To celebrate the wealth, she returned with proper baker's bread and bath buns oozing whipped cream.

As Caleb sank his teeth into the English delicacy, he felt himself relax . The money was beginning to roll in now instead of draining away. This cheque was the first of three and was his biggest earnings yet. Now, he could begin to feel like a proper farmer, growing profitable crops and earning a living. With similar substantial cheques, he could start investing in his farm instead of just scraping together the rent. He could look to the future. He could prove to his brothers that he could prosper away from the family's croft. He was thankful to Matthew for his help, Lydia for her kindness, Suzie for being Suzie, and especially to the Lord for arranging and overruling everything.

Suzie was disappointed when the apple picking finally came to an end. The barmy September weather, the quality and quantity of the fruit, the sizable bank cheque, and the congenial company had made the season a pleasure. Emerging from the kitchen after breakfast into the misty orchard, feeling the freshness of the early autumn air and observing the intricate, overnight lacemaking of thousands of spiders decorating the hedgerows and meadows filled her with energy and delight. But the highlight of each day was the journey to and from Milford Station.

Sitting together on the short bench of the cart, Suzie and Caleb trundled slowly through the winding Brookfield lanes. They were just perched high enough to enjoy a good view over the neighbouring farmers' hedges and to observe all the goings on. They passed hop gardens, chaotic with Eastend Londoners stripping the rough bines clean of hops, surrounded by prams, playing children, and elderly relatives on piles of coats. In the next field was an old couple bent double, laboriously digging up their potato harvest. Further still was a secluded meadow with sheep chewing the cud under the shade of an oak tree. Passing rows of cottages, they saw wives gathering in their dried washing, men working in their vegetable gardens, a young mother peeping in the pram at her sleeping baby, a toddler about to pull the tail of a sunbathing cat, and a milkmaid setting off to find her cows. Every now and again, they would be waved down by an elderly villager, who would then come hobbling to his gate to ask about the harvest and the family. Sometimes, for fear of missing the train, Caleb and Suzie had to politely cut short the rambling conversation, leaving the old gent leaning on his gate and watching the world go by.

There was never a risk of running out of topics for conversation. If they weren't talking about the apple crop, they were discussing the sheep. If they weren't passing observations about the scenes they encountered, they were recounting stories from their childhood. If they weren't discussing the previous Sunday's sermon, they debated the merits of psalms vs hymns. All the while, Suzie had the thrilling awareness of Caleb's close proximity—his trousered leg pressed against her skirt, his muscular arms against her sleeves, and his hobnail boots next to her clogs. In his presence, despite her working clothes, unflattering apron, and windswept hair, she felt more vibrantly feminine than she had ever felt before.

On one occasion, as they trundled home in the sunset, Suzie found herself softly singing:

Now the day is over,

Night is drawing nigh;

Shadows of the evening

Steal across the sky.

Suddenly feeling self-conscious, she stopped.

"Please go on, Suzie," urged Caleb gently. "That was beautiful."

Trying to remember all the words, she continued,

Now the darkness gathers,

Stars begin to peep,

Birds and beasts and flowers

Soon will be asleep.

Jesus, give the weary

Calm and sweet repose;

With Thy tend'rest blessing

May mine eyelids close.

Grant to little children

Visions bright of Thee;

Guard the sailors tossing

On the deep-blue sea.

By now, Caleb, having picked up the melody, was humming in a harmony of bass notes.

Comfort every sufferer

Watching late in pain;

Those who plan some evil

From their sin restrain.

Through the long night-watches

May Thine angels spread

Their white wings above me,

Watching round my bed.

Glory to the Father,

Glory to the Son,

And to Thee, blest Spirit,

While all ages run.

"Amen," their voices blended together as a fitting conclusion to the evening hymn. They jogged on in restful silence.

"Did you sing that to the two little Mortimer girls?" asked Caleb.

"Yes, I did, especially if one of them woke up frightened in the night."

"The tune is very soothing,"

"Yes."

"And you have a beautiful voice. I think…"

But Suzie never heard what he thought, for CharlieCharlie jumped out of the ditch to surprise them and beg for a ride home.

"You drive the old mare like an old man, Caleb!" he complained, "You plod along the road so slowly."

"We mustn't bruise the apples," explained Caleb.

"But you don't have any apples on the way back!"

"Maybe I just like talking to your sister then."

"Give me the reins, and I will show you what I call good drivining!" Charlie squeezed himself between them.

"Off you go then, lad," laughed Caleb, "but no using the whip!"

But now, all the rides to and from Milford were over. The apple baskets were brushed off and returned to the attics, the ladders to the barn, and Suzie felt flat. The Indian summer came to a chilly, damp end. The potato harvest was a stodgy, backbreaking task dominated by Charlie, who had managed to wiggle his way out of education for a few days to help. The sight of sacks of dry potatoes stored away with the apples they had kept for eating was the reward for this muddy, messy job. There was no surplus for selling.

And today was particularly vexing. Caleb had taken the afternoon off to learn hedge-laying with Mr Green. Bored of the job, Charlie moaned and groaned with every potato he turned. Lydia exasperatedly told him that he was definitely going to school tomorrow. Suzie's back ached from lugging sacks of spuds around.

167

She was fed up with the feel of dry soil on her hands and under her fingertips.

"Charlie!" she shouted. "You should have turned these potatoes! I want to bag them up, and they are still half wet!"

"I did them," retorted Charlie.

"You did not! Look at this!"

Lydia eased herself into an upright position.

"Charlie, you must stick to your job and turn the potatoes. If we bag them up wet, they will rot."

"Some are rotten already," grumbled Charlie, as if that were an excuse.

"Now, this lot will not be dry before the sun goes down and will be here all night. Thanks to you," spat Suzie.

"I'd better have tomorrow's school to help then."

"No, you will not!" cried Lydia and Suzie in unison.

Lydia left to prepare the meal, and Charlie disappeared with his catapult. Suzie was left to plod her way up the rows of dismantled potato hills. Self-pity flooded over her. She inwardly raged at John for his utter selfishness. She raged at her parents for not standing up to him. She raged at the inequalities of life. Only about a mile away, the darling daughters of Lord D'Egerton lived in the lap of luxury. Their pretty little fingers would never have been covered in soil, and their elegant backs would never have felt a sack of spuds. Yet, at any time, they could ring a bell and request a deep, hot bath to relax in. Suzie snorted at the very idea of such a bath for herself. All the hauling and boiling of water involved, then the palaver of emptying it afterwards, made it totally unrealistic.

Her anger turned again to John, then to men in general, to the hideous Mr Biggs, who was probably still secure in his post due to his obsequious behaviour. To Mr Mortimer who neglects his wife and daughters and wants to make an unpaid slave out of her. Then her rage turned to Caleb. She thought he was different, but he was probably just like the rest of them. Oh, it is fine to have a close friendship with a hardy, outdoor lass, but a wife? Oh no, not a working pony of a girl: what you need is an elegant showhorse. A pretty delicate little thing to admire as she does her fine needlework and arranges flowers. Caleb had been given ample opportunity to propose if he wanted to, so obviously, it wasn't his wish.

By now, Suzie had changed her task. Instead of picking up potatoes, she grabbed a fork and attacked the next potato plant. She plunged the fork into the ground and unearthed roots full of potatoes, she swiftly carried on digging down the row. She ignored the blisters developing on her hands, her aching back, and her thumping head. They merely echoed her inward misery. Her plaited hair had become loose, and as she wiped loose hairs away from her face, her soily hands left trails of dirt. She didn't care. No one else would care. She wanted to work until she collapsed into oblivion.

"Suzie, I've got the Weald of Kent Ram Sale catalogue!"

Suzie looked up and saw Caleb bounding towards her.

"All I want is a new Romney ram," she said flatly.

"But look, they have some Southdowns listed. I think we should try them."

"One of each, then?" suggested Suzie.

"I don't think we can afford that."

"Well, when I go next week, I can see which looks the best."

"I'll come too."

"I thought you said you wanted to go to the ploughing match."

"Well, I think I had better come."

"Don't you trust my judgement?" huffed Suzie.

"It's not that. There can be rough types there. Your father got me to promise I would look after you."

"Oh, I see." Suzie flung her fork onto the ground, turned on her heels, and stomped towards the meadow. "You're just nice to me to keep a promise to my father, are you?"

What a silly little fool I've been!

"Suzie, come back. It isn't like that at all."

Of course, it is like that! Now he will realise just how foolish I am!

She lurched her way over the potato hills. "At least I know where we stand now!" She was fighting back tears.

Caleb bounded after her.

"You are misunderstanding me, Suzie."

"I doubt it." She blundered over vegetable plants, tears blurring her vision.

"I don't want to fall out over a silly ram."

It's not just about a silly ram!

"I'm sorry you find yourself lumbered with the responsibility of looking after your working partner's incompetent daughter," she shouted over her shoulder. The heavy clay soil and her heavy heart impeded her flight.

Caleb stared at her in confusion. *Whatever is the problem? Incompetent!* Her capability was one of the innumerable qualities he admired in her. He ran after her and gained ground.

"Suzie, you don't realise —" He caught her by the arm. "You don't realise how much I love you."

Suzie stopped short and turned around. Surely she misheard him!?

Caleb grabbed her other arm and tenderly looked into her tear-stained face. "I love you, Suzie."

Suzie flopped her pounding head on his chest and burst into tears. She felt safe as he wrapped his arms around her. As he gently rubbed her back, her sobs subsided.

As she lifted up her wet and muddy face, she received her first kiss.

In the distance, Lydia could be heard calling that the meal was ready. They lingered, basking in their newly found joy, before reluctantly heading for the cottage. The sun had already sunk beneath the horizon, and they stumbled back through the uneven potato patch, hand in blistered hand. They stopped for a kiss at the garden gate and then again at the kitchen door.

Suzie reached for the door handle, but Caleb put out a hand to stop her.

"One minute, please," he said. "I haven't asked you to marry me yet."

Just as he got onto one knee, the door was flung open, knocking him sideways.

"Dinner is ready! NOW!" Charlie yelled into the darkness before slamming the door shut.

"Yes, I will," laughed Suzie as she helped him to his feet.

Stepping into the shadow and away from the dangerous door, they kissed again. Then they entered the kitchen to join the others.

"Whatever kept you both so long?" scolded Lydia as the pair washed their hands. "The food is getting cold."

"Sorry about that. I was just proposing something to Suzie, subject to Matthew's agreement, of course," Caleb casually replied, rubbing his hands in a towel.

"Potatoes or sheep?" asked Lydia with little interest.

Suzie giggled.

"Marriage, actually."

The effect was electrifying. Elsie clapped and laughed; Charlie danced a jig and Lydia beamed with pleasure. Suzie's head continued to throb, and she felt strangely distanced from reality. She didn't want to worry Caleb, so she returned his every smile. Underneath the headache and sore back, she was immensely happy.

It wasn't until she was lying in bed with a cold, wet cloth over her forehead that she remembered the sacks of potatoes she had left out in the night's dew.

CHAPTER 31

As Caleb fried his eggs and bacon for breakfast, he wondered if he was the happiest man in the country. Whistling under his breath, he counted his blessings. He had a faithful and loving Saviour who was the basis for his underlying peace. He had the loveliest and most suitable fiancée he could ever wish for. Matthew had written to give his blessing on the union but stipulated that the marriage should wait until he was home and available to walk his daughter down the aisle. He had money in his bank account and a flourishing farm. He looked around his bare kitchen and imagined all the feminine touches Suzie would add to his cottage. Definitely a tablecloth and curtains, and probably some daintier tableware. He imagined flowers on the windowsill and dried herbs hanging from the beams. He smiled to himself; under her loving touch, the cottage would be transformed into a proper home. Tish strolled up to him and looked expectantly towards the frying pan.

"And we will have to become civilised, my friend, won't we?"

Yesterday, Caleb and Suzie announced their engagement to the whole parish—they sat together in chapel. Instead of sitting in the family pew, Lydia had allowed Suzie to sit with him in his. In her best Sunday frock and wearing a beautiful new bonnet, Suzie looked elegant and demure. Caleb's heart swelled with love and pride as he walked her down the aisle and ushered her to their seat. He saw the ripple of elbow nudges and side glances as members of the congregation noticed the new seating arrangement and understood its significance.

Caleb let himself dream as he slowly ate his breakfast. With the next apple cheque that came in, he hoped to buy a cow, timber for another shed, and a double bed. Once Matthew had finished paying the wretched John's expenses and was back working on the farm, Suzie would be free to do housewifely tasks like butter making and apiculture when he got bees. Maybe they could run a small stall at the Milford market once a month, or so.. By working hard together, they should soon be able to put down a deposit on a small farm of their very own. Maybe they could even hire a farmhand. Caleb then imagined a busy household of little Bakers. Suzie would make a lovely mother. He smiled as he imagined her singing softly to their children at bedtime, making them feel snug and loved in the cosy cot he had made and under the thick blankets she had knitted.

Their engagement had caused a lot of excitement at the Baker steading. Enthusiastic well wishes had flooded in from his parents and brothers and sisters-in-law. Promises of visits, home-made quilts, and family recipes filled the letters. The Highland women felt their homemaking skills were what all wives should aspire to. They flooded Suzie with nuggets of well-meaning advice. Caleb smiled as he thought of the predictable jokes his brothers had passed—all faithfully recorded in his mother's letters. Some said he was marrying the daughter to keep on good terms with the motherly Lydia. Others joked that he was still too wet behind the ears to wed. Others wondered if Tish would be banished to a kennel. Reuben wondered how Suzie's Gaelic lessons were coming on. But, in their own teasing way, one and all were delighted for him and looked forward to welcoming another sister-in-law into the family. Maybe, Caleb mused. He could take his bride to the Highlands for a little honeymoon, as well as introduce his Mrs Baker to all the other Mrs Bakers and the whole clan. He longed to show her all his childhood haunts. She would find the rugged landscape captivating. He should put some of the apple money aside for that—maybe foregoing the Southdown ram. The thought of rams brought him back to the present moment. Today was the Weald of Kent Ram Sale.

As Caleb stepped out into the blustery chill of the late October day, it contrasted favourably with a Scottish autumn. As yet, there hadn't been a frost in Kent, yet in the Highlands, they had already experienced weeks of freezing weather and were bedding down for another long, hard winter. Down south, the elements felt less threatening, the winters felt less daunting, and the ground seemed more fruitful.

Caleb built a pen out of sheep hurdles on the cart and then harnessed up Chestnut. Her warm breath tickled his face. He patted her on the neck, and she nuzzled towards him.

"Good morning, you two!" Suzie called out as she crossed the farmyard. She petted Chestnut and kissed Caleb. She was wearing a smart-fitted coat and a brown bonnet.

"You look quite the businesswoman," commented Caleb admiringly.

"It is from deep in Ma's wardrobe," Suzie explained. "It is hard to know what to wear to a ram sale—if you are a woman."

"You look just the part."

"You don't look bad yourself, in your smarter work jacket and flat cap. All you need now is a straw sticking out of your mouth," teased Suzie as she pushed a promising-looking lunch basket under the waggon bench. She had even remembered a carriage rug.

"You're mothering me already, Suzie," joked Caleb as she tucked them in.

"I hope I never mother you—that sounds a bit bossy."

"Wife me, then?" suggested Caleb

"Yes, but why has no one come up with that expression before 'Wife-ing?'"

"I think we have just coined it."

As they jogged along behind Chestnut, snuggly huddled beneath the woollen wrap, they discussed wedding plans. With money from the next apple cheque, Lydia would buy material for the wedding dress. Suzie and her mother had already enjoyed many hours discussing the cut, the style, and the line. Caleb was relieved that it would all be kept a secret from him—he didn't want to be involved in long debates about tucks, frills, or lace.

The conversation then moved on to buying Caleb's cow. Suzie thought he should invest in two. She looked forward to improving her diary skills—milking, straining, and churning. Caleb said he would buy her a marble table for the cellar for butter making. She wanted to try her hand at producing cheese. Suzie suggested that, in view of his fondness for the Highland cattle he'd sold off to come south, maybe he should think about a beef herd, too. The apple cheques had been used numerous times before they had reached the Weald Ram Sale.

The auction field was already filled with waggons when they arrived. The movement of sheep, horses, wheels, and boots was already taking its toll on the muddy grass. Having tethered up Chestnut, Caleb and Suzie joined the steam of shepherds making their way to the rows of sheep pens. As they pushed their way nearer the pens, the musky scent of the rams mingled with the odour of stale male sweat. Suzie glanced around and realised she was the only female in sight. She was pleased Caleb hadn't gone to the ploughing match. They were jostled along the pens, stopping to admire the curly-fleeced Cotswolds, the black-faced Dorset Downs, the curly-horned Shetlands, and the cuddly-looking Dartmoors. As she paused to give the Dartmoor ram a stroke, Suzie realised she had become separated from Caleb. Once she had lost her male companion, she became an oddity in the eyes of the farmers. Younger men ogled her, and older men stared. She was unsure whether they approved of her presence there or thought she was intruding on a male event.

"Look at this beauty," Leered a scruffy shepherd to his friends, "misread Ram Sale for Pram Sale, did ya?"

Another man purposely bumped into her, "What time are you going on auction, me love?"

Enjoying the joke, another man added,

"What's your starting bid, then, sweetheart?"

Suzie felt panic rising. Everywhere were big, menacing men, but no Caleb. The Southdowns! She would walk towards the Southdowns; that was the breed he wanted. The Southdown rams were so cute, with wide noses, smiley faces, and stocky bodies, but Suzie wasn't in the mood to admire and pet them. They were surrounded by another crowd of high-spirited men, ready to bait each other on with crude comments towards her. The Romneys! She had wanted a Romney ram—maybe he was at their pen. She weaved her way towards them.

"Suzie!"

Suzie had never heard such a welcome sound as Caleb's voice at that moment.

"Are you alright?" asked Caleb as she took his arm.

"Fine, thanks," she answered. Even a decent man like Caleb would probably never understand the challenges of being a woman, so she decided not to waste her breath.

"I thought you would be admiring the Southdowns."

Caleb shook his head. "Let's just have one ram this year." He wasn't going to tell her about the honeymoon idea yet. "Let's stick to Romneys."

The Romney auction was late in the day. To keep entertained, Caleb and Suzie went to watch the auctioneer sell the Shetlands. His rapid, fire-filled chant was awe-inspiring. Hardly pausing for a breath, he raced through the numbers, pointing his wooden hammer at the bidders, who were barely moving a muscle as they placed their bids. A raise of the eyebrow here, a nod there, a wave of the catalogue somewhere else, then "going, going, gone!" BANG! "Sold to the man with the moustache." BANG! The couple were amused at the way the auctioneer so aptly described the highest bidder of each ram: "Sold to the man with no front teeth…the man with hairy nostrils…to my old friend from Mill Farm," and so it went.

"How will he describe you?" teased Suzie

"Me? Don't you want to do the bidding?"

"I'd very much prefer not to," shuddered Suzie. "Anyway, he would probably overlook my waves, winks or head nods, thinking I was just an onlooker."

The auctioneer's chant was interesting, but the prices were shocking. Twenty-six shillings! That was more than four weeks' wages for a farm labourer.

Despondently wandering a little further, they found a man selling roasted chestnuts. The smell was so appetising that they bought a cone-full each. As they stood nibbling, they eavesdropped. It was clear that the auctioneer was not the only one doing business that day.

"Aye, me ram is a grand fella. I don't wonna get rid of 'im, but 'e's te father of all me ewes."

"Did ya bring 'im 'ere today?"

"Na, I'm just 'ere te buy not sell."

"We'll, I'd be interested in 'im. Fifteen?"

"Deal! Come over en pick 'im up when ya can."

Caleb and Suzie exchanged an interested nod.

To their left was another conversation.

"'Tis all very well, buying a decent ram, but they lose condition so fast. So do me ewes."

"Don't ya give em apple cider vinegar?"

"Ya wot?"

"Yeah, give em a drench of the stuff, and they keep in good nick."

Another glance and nod were exchanged.

"Let's head back to the Romney Ram area and see if we can have a bit of useful conversation there," Caleb suggested.

"Just what I was thinking," agreed Suzie.

Several men were leaning on the sheep hurdles of the Romney pens. Some were prodding the rams, inspecting their physics or their teeth. One older chap was absorbed in petting and muttering to a friendly sheep.

"I reckon you were a sock lamb, hey? Brought up on a bottle, were ya? You're a nice lad, aren't ya?"

Caleb and Suzie sided up to him and leant on the gate.

"He's a nice chap, isn't he?" commented Caleb.

"Aye, I know a nice ram when I see one. Nice nature, I be meaning," agreed the old man. "Rams can be as soppy as a kitten if ya treat 'em well. But ya must never fully trust 'em. That broad fore'ead of em could kill ya," he said, rubbing the ram's head. Caleb rubbed it too.

"Are you local?" Suzie asked.

"Aye, I'm from the other side of Brookfield, over Silver Green way."

"You like Romneys; I take it," ventured Caleb.

"Aye, ya can't beat a good Romney. Te ewes are good mothers, te lambs make good meat, te wool is quality, and te top it all, they look beautiful."

"I agree completely."

"Did your old ram die?" Suzie asked innocently.

"Aye, no." The man shook his head. "Me ram is free."

"Free?" interrupted Caleb.

179

"Aye, free years old and fighting fit, but I can't breed 'im wiv 'is daughters, can I? I've come to get new blood in me stock."

"Have you sold your other ram?" Caleb asked.

"Na, I'm loath to, cos 'e is like a pet te me, I 'ave to admit. But I need te. Them prices today are a bit 'igher than I was bargaining for."

"What is your selling price?"

The old man looked surprised.

"We need a nice, friendly Romney, as there are still youngsters on the farm. We have a soft spot for friendly rams too." Suzie stopped herself from pushing any more.

The man looked them full in the face, one after another, then began to smile.

"Well, I reckon me Roger—that's what I call 'im, would be going te a good 'ome." 'Ow does twelve shillings sound te you?"

"That sounds fine!" Caleb and Suzie said it in unison.

Caleb and the man shook hands. Caleb handed over the money, and the man gave them his address. "I 'ope to see ya next week," he said. "'Arvey's me name."

"And I hope you can buy this friendly chap, Mr Arvey," replied Suzie.

"I reckon I will." The man lowered his voice and said , "E's a bit smaller tan t'others, so I 'ope for a bargain. Twill be at te end of te day, and I's 'oping te auctioneer will be ready for 'is evening cigar and sherry, and not want te 'ang around te drum up te price."

"I hope so, too."

Caleb and Suzie congratulated themselves on their shrewd business sense as they rode away from the auction field.

"Will the packed lunch keep until tomorrow?" Caleb asked after a pause in the conversation.

"Yes, it is just slices of savoury pie and apples. Why do you ask?"

"I was thinking we have saved a bit of time, leaving the auction early, so why don't we stop off at Milford and have lunch in a tearoom? It's a bit too chilly to stop for a picnic."

Suzie was excited—they had never done that sort of thing before.

"That sounds lovely!" she exclaimed, "But what about our muddy boots?"

"Let's stop and wipe them on the grass verge," and so they did.

"I might just call in at the lumber yard while we are in town."

"What do you want timber for?" asked Suzie.

"Our double bed," replied Caleb, smiling.

Suzie blushed deeply.

"Unless you prefer single beds, of course," he teased.

"No, thanks."

"Phew," he whistled.

Holding the reins with just one hand, he reached out and wrapped his other arm around Suzie's shoulders. She snuggled into him.

"Are you in full control of the moving vehicle, Mr Baker?" she asked in a deep, authoritative voice.

"Full control, Constable, and look, I can even do this too." And with that, he planted a kiss on her cheek.

It felt so novel, sitting in a smart tearoom with Caleb. With his handsome looks and good manners, no one would accuse him of looking out of place. Suzie was proud to be at his side. They were shown to a little roundtable by an open fire and served by smartly dressed waitresses. Caleb's workman's hands looked huge as he drank Chinese tea from the delicate teacup and assembled his scone with jam and cream with a little ivory-handled knife.

As the warmth of the fire hit them, Suzie began to become suspicious.

"Are we beginning to give off the smell of the ram sale?" she hissed to Caleb.

"I rather think we are," he said. They both giggled.

Suzie remembered the shame and embarrassment she and the other Brookfield children felt at school when their clothes gave off rural smells. But now, she felt no shame. She and Caleb were proud of their farming activities. Milford may mock as it wished, but she would hold her head high, knowing she was helping to keep the nation fed.

Having had an elegant sufficiency, the pair paid up and left the tea room.

"That was very nice; thank you, darling," said Suzie as they parted at the street. While Caleb was at the lumber yard, she would visit the haberdashery shop to browse through their lace. Having feasted her eyes on the bewildering selection, she wandered down the high street towards the lumber yard.

"Good afternoon, Miss Griffen," called out a familiar voice.

Suzie looked around.

"Oh, good afternoon, Maggie. How are you?"

"Particularly well, thanking you."

"That's good."

"Yes. 'Ave you not 'eard?"

"Heard what, Maggie?"

"I'm becoming Mrs Mortimer next week." Maggie's face was alight with delight.

"Oh!" Suzie felt speechless.

"Yeah, 'e finally saw sense and knew I was the one for 'im."

"I wish you every happiness," Suzie stammered.

"And 'e's such a sweet'eart that 'e's allowing me muver to come en live wiv us. Them girls love 'er like a grandmuver."

"That's nice."

"I don't 'ave te worry about money no more. Nor me damp 'ouse."

"How nice!"

"Ya missed out there, didn't ya?"

Suzie opened her mouth to reply, but Maggie had already walked off in an air of smugness.

CHAPTER 32

Suzie bounced into the kitchen to share the day's events with her mother, but one look at Lydia's face told her that all was not well.

"Ma, you look so pale. Are you ill?"

"No, Suzie. Come to the table and look at this." Lydia's voice was flat.

With trepidation, Suzie crossed the room and looked at the offending paperwork.

"A banker's cheque of only forty shillings?" she gasped. "Surely that isn't the grand total?"

"Read the letter."

Suzie picked up the letter and took it to the light of the window.

Mr Griffen

Market flooded with French Fruit . Price collapsed. Apples sold to brewery for cider.

Yours faithfully

"Oh, dear!" Suzie signed as she flopped into a chair. She felt physically weak as a heavy cloud of gloom submerged her.

"I need to tell Caleb," she said at last, trying to rally her limp limbs into action.

"No, you stay put," ordered Lydia. "I can tell him. I have had a bit longer to take in the news."

Suzie felt too crushed to argue.

The evening meal was a gloomy affair.

"French fruit?" CharlieCharlie protested, "Isn't that illegal?"

"It's called a free market," Caleb explained ruefully.

"It seems so strange," mused Suzie. "We were so careful about finger marks when picking. We were so careful trundling them along to the train station. Then the French fruit, whatever it was, comes in, having been jolted about over the English Channel, and people prefer them."

"There is no loyalty," sighed Elsie.

"Had we known, we could have sent them straight to a brewery and saved paying the middleman, Mr whats-his-name, Flockhart," grumbled Caleb.

"I wish we had stuck to the Milford market," Suzie mumbled.

Caleb looked defensive.

"No one was to know," Lydia quickly replied to deflect any tension. "Farming is all about trial and error. Often at no fault of the farmer."

"If it isn't the weather, it is disease. If it isn't disease, it is the market."

Lydia had never heard Caleb be quite so negative. She felt for the poor lad. So much had hung on the cheque for him—his farming and marital plans, and his pride.

"At least you still have some fat lambs to sell," she encouraged him.

"Humph."

"'Shall we receive good at the hand of God, and shall we not receive evil?'" Lydia quoted softly.

Everyone was silent.

"Thank you, Lydia," Caleb smiled at her with tear-filled eyes. "Job was a farmer, too."

Caleb went home straight after the meal. Suzie had hoped to talk to him alone, but the 'do not disturb' expression on his face and his abrupt departure indicated that he was in no mood for discussion.

Suzie went to bed early and cried herself to sleep.

The next morning, her youthful optimism had returned. Her parents had weathered tough farming years and bleak times. They didn't need big plans or profits. If the farm ticked over and they had enough food to survive, that sufficed. She kept busy all morning with routine chores. Normally, she would have crossed tracks with Caleb by now. She felt he was avoiding her. She toyed with the idea of hunting him down but decided he probably needed a bit of time alone. She understood men can be like that. She spent a few hours collecting cob nuts. Everyone would enjoy the succulent treat. But by mid-afternoon, she was determined to find Caleb. They needed to talk, whether he wanted to or not.

As she crossed the paddock and entered his farm, the regular thud of an axe became audible and guided her to his location. A huge pile of chopped logs and his discarded jacket indicated he had been hard at work for several hours.

"You've been productive," Suzie hesitantly commented.

Without acknowledging her presence, Caleb picked up the next log and split it in two with one hefty blow.

"It won't generate any money, though. Will it?" Caleb challenged.

"But it will generate heat, and that is important." Suzie tried to sound bright. "It isn't all about money."

"Not all about money?" Thud! "No, it isn't all about money, is it?" Thud! "But how else do you suggest we buy a cow?" Thud! "Or a marble tabletop for butter making?" Thud! "Or pay for a marriage license?" THUD!

He stopped, leant on the axe. "Suzie, we'll have to forget this marriage idea."

Suzie felt weak. "No, we don't," she croaked.

"I don't want you to be dragged into poverty by a peasant farmer. I don't want you starving yourself to feed our children or working yourself to the bone to make ends meet." Caleb picked up another massive block. THUD!

"You aren't dragging me into this. I am in this already. And I am not complaining!" Caleb's despair made Suzie stronger.

"You'd have been better off marrying morose Mortimer."

"Rubbish! I'd prefer to be a subsistence farmer with you than marry someone like that."

"There's no glamour in poverty, Suzie."

"You don't need to tell me about poverty, Caleb Baker. I've lived through many years of it with my family. But they don't quit, so I see no reason to give up either. We don't need a huge bank balance to get by."

"But we can't marry anyway, Suzie. Thanks to your useless brother." Thud!

"What do you mean?"

Caleb leant on his axe again, "Don't you get it?" he asked in an air of exasperation. "Life isn't as simple as you think. Your father now needs to continue longer with the railways. The apple money might have been enough for him to finish with them and still pay John's fees, but now it certainly isn't. So, your labour is required on the farm. We can't afford to hire a farmhand."

"I can work when I am married. I fully intend to."

"Life doesn't work like that, Suzie. In the normal course of events, you might soon be expecting our baby and then be a mother. Your role will change."

Suzie blushed. Caleb spoke of their baby in a matter-of-fact way he might use to discuss rams and ewes.

"Until the John fees are fully paid or the farms make money, I don't think we can marry," Caleb stated glumly but decidedly.

Suzie's brain was racing around, trying to come up with solutions, but Caleb's bleak logic seemed unarguably realistic.

"Then I will wait and wait for as long as it takes."

Caleb looked so despondent and crushed. Feeling a huge wave of love and pity for him, Suzie rushed towards him and wrapped him in her arms, axe, and all. As she rubbed his back, Caleb's tense body eventually relaxed against hers. He slumped his head onto her shoulder and let out a heartfelt groan. *If only men would cry,* thought Suzie, *it would do them a world of good.*

"Let's go to your kitchen, and I'll make a pot of tea," she suggested tentatively.

"Tea doesn't solve anything."

"But it helps most things."

"The stove isn't lit."

188

"Don't worry, I know where to find plenty of firewood." She grinned at him, and she was rewarded with a weak smile in return.

CHAPTER 33

Just as they were about to load Roger the ram from the stable onto the cart, the heavens opened. Observing the sky from the doorway, Mr Arvey predicted it wouldn't be a short shower. He seemed delighted that his visitors would need to delay their departure and invited them into his cottage to meet his wife.

Rain lashed against the windowpanes, and the wind whistled under the back door, but the inclemency of the outside only made the cottage kitchen feel snugger. Mrs Harvey (she soon informed them she was not Mrs Arvey) welcomed Caleb and Suzie into her house and set the kettle on to boil.

Sitting around the cluttered kitchen table, they enjoyed tea and toasted teacakes. The Harvey's sheepdog contentedly slumbered on a mat before the range. The odours of wet dog, rams' musk, and toast filled the small room. As the rain poured, the conversation flowed.

"Baker?" exclaimed Mr Harvey. "You say ya name is Baker?"

"That's right," nodded Caleb.

"I knew a Baker—a real knowledgeable shepherd. What was 'is name, Ma?"

"John Baker."

"Ahh, of course, and you 'ad a shine for 'im, didn't ya? 'Till I swept ya off ya feet."

He teased his wife.

"He is my father," stated Caleb.

"Well, I never!" Mr Harvey leaned over the table and squeezed Caleb's shoulder. "Well, I never. And now I'm selling 'is son my ram. Well, I never did!"

The family history of the Bakers was discussed, and then the D'Egertons became the focus of the conversation.

"We 'ardly see 'em now, do we Ma?" Mr Harvey grumbled. "Tey used te reside at te big 'ouse most of te time, but we aint good enough for em no more. Only ya dear Lady Isabel."

"Ahh, yes, poor dear," Mrs Harvey spoke tenderly, "I still see her once a week, up at the dowager house. She even sends me her carriage to ride in. You see, I was her maid for many a year…"

"For far too many a year," her husband interrupted.

Mrs Harvey smiled wryly. "Mr Harvey here wanted to wed me," she explained, "but poor Lady Isabel couldn't do without me. She was very low. Her son had just left for boarding school, and her husband, well, how can I put it? He didn't keep to his wedding vows, if you know what I mean?"

Caleb and Suzie nodded.

"So, it was six years before we could get wed."

"At least," interjected her husband.

"But I still think we did the right thing. At least I was still of an age to have children. I know some poor women who have had to wait for marriage as they look after their parents or some such thing, and by the time they tie the knot, they are beyond childbearing age," Mrs Harvey said as she refilled the teapot. "And Lady Isabel, bless her, has never forgotten our sacrifice. We've never had to pay rent, and a small salary is paid to us every month without fail. She is the kindest sort you could ever wish to meet."

Caleb looked at Suzie, who had decided to keep her mouth shut.

"Next time I see her, I'll tell her about a Baker being down here. She is always talking about Scotland and her parents' old estates. I think she prefers thinking about the distant past to the present. Between you and me." And now, Mrs Harvey was talking in hushed tones, "I don't think she likes the goings on of her family. She grieves at their ungodly living. They are more interested in stocks and shares than agriculture. I don't know what will happen when she passes. I really don't."

"What is there in the way of family?" Suzie asked, "I should really know, but I've forgotten."

"Emily, her first daughter, married 'below herself', as they would say. But he was, and is, a nice man. They live in the west of the country and have three daughters and a son. Emily is the only one I sometimes see visiting her mother. From what I understand, they are godfearing people and give Lady Isabel comfort rather than heartache. Amelia, the middle child, met some rich, showy heir during the social season she was presented in London. Lady Isabel was most grieved by her choice. They live somewhere near Oxford. I believe the marriage hasn't been the most loyal affair. They have two sons and a daughter." As Mrs Harvey spoke, she was toasting more teacakes at the range. Pulling each one off the long fork, she passed them to Suzie for buttering.

"Of course, you both know about Geoffrey, the only son. Lord D'Edgerton, he is now. Inherited it all."

"Nothing like 'is mother, is 'e?" tutted Mr Harvey.

"Not one bit!" His wife shook her head sadly. "She'd send gifts to tenants when their wives gave birth, send condolences if someone died, and always give a generous hamper at Christmas."

"But we never 'ear from 'im. Or 'is foreign wife."

"He married an Italian," explained Mrs Harvey.

"Roman Catholic," added Mr Harvey.

"One son and three daughters, all living the high life," Mrs Harvey sat down and took a bite from her teacake.

"They've even been to New York." She looked gravely at Caleb and Suzie as if to assure herself they understood the excessive vulgarity of their lifestyle. They duly shook their heads in sadness.

Suzie looked out the now misted-up window. The rain had stopped. She nudged Caleb's knee with her own.

"Well, we've had a lovely wee time with you, but it looks as if the shower is over, so we'd better not delay you good folks any longer but be on our way," Caleb said, standing up. Before they left the farm, Mrs Harvey loaded them with eggs and a pot of pickled cucumbers.

"And you now know where we are. Drop in anytime. We like having visitors."

"We will!" agreed Suzie sincerely.

"Six years!" sighed Caleb as they turned the corner.

"At least!" Suzie added grimly.

CHAPTER 34

Looking back on the winter, Lydia thought it blurred into one long memory of waiting and hard work. She was waiting for Matthew's contract with the railway line company and John's indenture to be completed. Suzie and Caleb were waiting for marriage. Elsie was waiting and cajoling to be allowed to leave school. Charlie, what was he waiting for? Probably nothing more consequential than his next meal.

Days were filled from beginning to end with housework and sewing. Queen Victoria created a new fashion by having twelve bridesmaids. Now, each bride seemed determined to outdo her peers in the number of attendants she required. As Gwendoline's reputation for wedding apparel grew and her business became overwhelmed with exacting brides and their doting mothers, she came up with an astute solution. She conducted the initial consultation, and then, once the pattern and fabrics were decided upon, her trusted team of workers measured up all the girls and cut the cloth. Parcels of fabrics, lace, thread, and detailed patterns were then sent across to Lydia in Kent. Lydia then completed the dresses and sent them back for Gwendoline to do a final fitting and make any minor adjustments. Lydia enjoyed the work. The clientele was affluent, the fabrics were luxurious, the patterns intricate, and the wages generous. Whenever a new parcel arrived, she and Elsie were like little girls at Christmas as they gleefully opened the layers of packaging and admired the contents. They wondered if they would ever get used to the extravagance of the upper classes.

Alongside this enterprise, Lydia still fulfilled requests from villagers for repairs, alterations, and the making of new dresses. Having a space dedicated to her work had proved to be such a good idea. The finer fabrics never left her sewing room for fear of soiling, but she took the homely rough spun garments of her neighbours to the armchair at the kitchen stove during the evenings. Her spectacles were invaluable when she worked her new machine or stitched by hand. The light colours of the bridesmaid's dresses suited her eyes much better than the dark hues of mourning garb. The children discouraged her from working into the evening, but when she did, Suzie and Caleb insisted she spend some of her earnings on a bigger, more elegant pair of oil lamps. They gave off a delightfully large sphere of light.

Matthew had come home for Christmas. He had looked well, despite a marked limp, and was very smart in his office outfit. Lydia was delighted to see him looking less gaunt and careworn, but a small part of her was jealous that it was another woman who had provided the meals and laundered his clothes. An even smaller part of her was slightly annoyed that his life was so much simpler than hers. He had only himself and his work to worry about, while she had to juggle the cares and concerns of the whole family. She wanted to be cheerful and welcoming, and she certainly succeeded, but she also didn't want him to leave with the impression that life for her was a bed of roses. Then again, she didn't want him to leave, feeling guilty that she was under too much strain. She wanted him to feel missed, to know he was still needed, but also that she was coping. So many wants and so many contradictory wishes, but her overriding wish and prayer was for him to soon return for good and slot back into the family with ease and cheerfulness.

Lydia silently observed Caleb and Suzie. They worked hard and well, but they lacked bounce. Most of the chores during the winter were what Matthew called 'Not a ha'penny' tasks—they had to be done but did not produce any income. Hedges had to be trimmed, orchards needed pruning, tools and barns needed repairing, logs needed chopping, and animals needed tending. At least, thanks to the visiting threshing machine, that dusty and laborious task no longer dominated windy days. The two of them had visited Mr and Mrs Harvey a few times socially, but they also earned some money by helping them pluck and gut the gaggle of geese they had fattened up for the Christmas market. They both hated the task and got chilblained feet and raw hands from standing in a draughty barn and handling wet, chilly innards, but the extra money before Christmas provided a few welcome luxuries for the family. They also received two plump geese as a thank-you gift.

Whenever Caleb heard of a local farmer requiring extra labourers for a project, he went along, leaving Suzie to run their farms. He could command a wage almost twice that of a woman's, so it made commercial sense for them. Suzie understood this but also felt that she missed out socially by not being able to join in with the teamwork.

"But they wouldn't have accepted me as part of the team, anyway," she rationalised. "They don't want women interfering in their work—unless she is offering to make the tea."

Lydia sometimes worried that her daughters worked so hard that they had little time for friendships with other local girls. Were they being deprived? They never mentioned a longing for more buddies and did not seem to expect it. Looking around at her neighbours and their families, she realised that most people had little time to cultivate friendships. Girls in service rarely had time off, while those working in Milford were away from home from dawn till dusk. She had always been too busy to feel lonely. Maybe they had inherited contentment with their own company from both her and Matthew. She was pleased that Elsie had recently discovered the joys of reading. Miss Milton had used her charms and contacts to enlist sponsors for a small lending library at the school. Elsie was so delighted with the book corner that Miss Milton appointed her the chief librarian. An understanding and appreciation of each other was developing, thanks to their shared interest in literature. Lydia hoped they could keep Elsie in school a little longer.

John was a vexing subject. His selfish actions and their ramifications upon the whole family irked everyone, but they particularly irritated Caleb. Lydia understood why it should niggle him. He had never met John, yet his behaviour and the poor apple price had impacted Caleb's plans so negatively. Caleb had a cheerful and optimistic outlook on life, but he would pass a sour comment now and again when he had had a hard and tiring day. Lydia saw that these remarks hurt Suzie, who was equally powerless to do anything about their situation.

"Would you like me to write to John and explain how we are having to postpone your wedding plans?" Lydia asked the couple one evening.

"Father wouldn't like that."

"I think he should be informed of the state of affairs," Caleb contradicted.

"But could it change anything, anyway?" Suzie replied doubtfully.

"Maybe not, but I still think he should know."

So Lydia wrote, and John replied. His letter was long and rambling, but the gist of it was that it was nice for Suzie that she had a marriage to look forward to, when for the likes of him, all hope of marriage to his true love had been dashed due to the heartless prejudice of her parents. Lydia slipped the letter into the stove—it would only antagonise Caleb yet further against his brother-in-law-to-be.

As January gave way to February, Caleb became more withdrawn, and Lydia worried. Back in the autumn, he had moved his bed into the kitchen to save on fuel. But now, his unused rooms were damp and musty. All his clothes smelt of mould, and he seemed to have a permanent cold. Suzie's attempts to jolly him along were unsuccessful. Her potions and concoctions to remedy his ailments were gratefully received but futile. He worked as hard and diligently as ever, but in a plodding and joyless manner. Instead of being the life and soul of the party around the stove in the evenings, he often apologetically excused himself and went straight to bed.

Just before the lambing season started, Matthew returned home. The Sharpthorne Tunnel was complete, and the team had disbanded. It was lovely to have him back for good and to have his wise advice and steady hand at the helm. His relief and pleasure at being home were felt by all. His admiration for Lydia's shrewd business sense and intricate needlework meant more to her than all the notes of thanks she received from grateful customers. His help with the farm chores eased Suzie's load and gave her hope for better days. She, like him, tried to ignore the fact that he was slower than he used to be and far less agile.

Matthew had only been home for a week when Caleb sought him out.

"I wanted to catch you alone, Mr Griffen," he said, his face solemn and drawn.

"What's up, lad?" Matthew asked kindly.

"I've made a hash of keeping your business running in your absence, and I want to apologise."

"Rubbish!" exclaimed Matthew. "You have done a good job. The apple price was completely outside your control. I am grateful for all you have done."

Caleb ignored the praise.

"I need to give up my farm, Matthew. I am behind with the rent. I don't know how to tell Suzie."

Matthew felt overwhelming sympathy for the poor, despondent lad.

"Lydia's business is doing fairly well. I am sure we can scrape together to help you out, son."

Caleb shook his head.

"I don't want to be a drain to you. You don't need another family member sapping you of money."

The men stared at the muddy ground between them. Caleb was squishing his boot into a ridge to join two puddles together.

"So, what are your plans?" Matthew asked.

"I will see lambing out, then go back home."

"And Suzie?"

"If she is willing to wait for me to get on my feet again, I would be most grateful, for I love her dearly. But I would understand if she decided she could do better with someone else."

"She would wait, I'm sure." Matthew tried to encourage him.

"You can never be sure with women," Caleb answered ruefully.

When Suzie heard the news, she crumbled. All winter, she had stayed strong. She had made herself strong for her mother, her younger siblings, and especially Caleb, but now, it all drained away.

Everything drained away: her energy, optimism, and spiritual peace. Did God really care for her? Did she really have faith? The minister preached a sermon about the sower and the seed. He explained that the outcome for the seeds on the rocks, shallow ground, and thistles was all the same. Maybe she was a seed amongst the thistles—the cares of this world would sap any life from her, and she would be exposed as a counterfeit on the day of judgement. Her inward joy evaporated.

Caleb reassured her over and over again that his love for her was unwavering and his decision to go home was to get back on his feet as soon as possible and then marry her. Lying in bed, Suzie imagined him meeting childhood chums from the highlands, realising the complexity of a long-distance relationship, settling down into the loving embrace of his family, and soon forgetting her.

She pondered alternative plans. She could get paid work to pay his rent, but his pride would not allow for that. She could marry him and go with him, but it was clear to all involved that her Pa could not cope alone any longer. She was torn between her family and her fiancé. Caleb knew that and had taken the decision away from her. She half-resented that. Now, every day was both precious and painful for the couple. They clung to each other with a new intensity, knowing that a long separation was creeping nearer and nearer.

"I wish lambing would go on forever," Suzie whispered into Caleb's ear as she sat on his knee in the sheep barn.

"And so do I!" signed Caleb, tickling her cheek with his stubbled chin.

CHAPTER 35

"Caleb! Suzie! Come QUICKLY!"

Still covered with mucous and blood from a difficult delivery, Caleb and Suzie rushed out of the barn towards the house. Suzie feared something had happened to Pa. Why else would Ma shout so loudly and urgently?

"There's a D'Edgerton carriage out the front, and the coachman said that Mr Caleb Baker and Miss Suzannah Griffen are summoned for an audience."

"Why?" they asked in unison as they frantically cleaned their forearms with ice-cold water.

"He gave no explanation."

"I'd better go and see him," decided Caleb. "Maybe it is about me giving notice of the tenancy last week."

"I'll quickly get changed," called Suzie as she ran upstairs. "But why would they want me?"

Caleb was soon back. "The man has no idea why we are wanted, but he told me to put on better clothes but be nippy about it." He explained this to Lydia before sprinting across the paddock towards his cottage.

"I forgot to ask Pa to keep an eye on that new lamb," sighed Suzie as they bounced around on the springy seats of the handsome cab.

They jogged along in silence. Caleb ran through all possible reasons for the summons. Would he be evicted immediately? Or maybe they wanted to offer him a grace period?

"The Lord God omnipotent reigneth," he quoted aloud.

"The king's heart is in the hands of the Lord," replied Suzie. They grasped hands and smiled weakly.

"This isn't the main drive to the big house," exclaimed Suzie as the carriage turned a corner.

"You are at the Dowager House," explained the coachman as he lowered the steps for them to disembark.

Mystified, the couple headed for the front door. They were relieved of their coats in a spacious, marble-floored hallway, then ushered into the morning room and the presence of Lady Isabel. They stammered their polite greetings and were shown to their seats. The noblewoman looked like a diminutive figure as she sat, cushioned and wrapped in a large, winged armchair.

"Tea and drop scones, please, Martha," she requested in a frail but authoritative voice. The maid bobbed a curtsy and left.

"I understand from Mrs Harvey that you are John Baker's son," Lady Isabel said, peering intently at him through lorgnette spectacles.

"That is correct," confirmed Caleb.

"So, you grew up in Taitneach?"

"Yes, indeed."

Suzie watched as Caleb and the old lady became animated and cheerful as they discussed the little town, its church, the little streets,

202

and then the scenery surrounding it. *No wonder Caleb wants to return,* she thought.

The room was warm. The sun beamed through a big bay window, and a large fire burned steadily in the ornate hearth. The musty smell of Caleb's best suit began to pervade the elegant morning room. Lady Isabel reached for her smelling salts.

"A bheil Gàidhlig agad?" she asked him.

"Tha, tha mi deònach," Caleb replied, smiling. The old woman's pale face beamed with happiness.

Suzie listened to the lilting sounds of the Gaelic language and felt even further removed from her fiancé. She sighed to herself. *All that haste away from the busy lambing barn just to pass the time of day with this entitled old lady who has no idea of the hardships we are going through. How irritating! And she has probably completely forgotten the injustice she did to me!*

"Were you taught the metrical psalms?"

"Aye, as a wee bairne," smiled Caleb as he threw another log onto the fire.

"Then sing Psalm 46 with me," commanded Lady Isabel.

God is our refuge and our strength,

in straits a present aid;

Therefore, although the earth remove,

we will not be afraid:

Lady Isabel's shrill singing voice blended with Caleb's rich tones as they sang through the first few verses. At one stage, a maid put her head around the door to check that all was well, but on seeing her mistress looking so happy and absorbed, she smiled at Suzie and quietly closed the door. Suzie enjoyed the psalm but couldn't help wondering whether her father was coping with the lambing and whether the new, weak lamb had found milk yet. The short nights caught up with her, and the stuffy room made her drowsy.

Lady Isabel must have felt the same. Having elongated the last note of the fifth verse to indicate that was enough, she closed her eyes with a sign of contentment and leaned back against the cushions. Suzie glanced at Caleb. It looked suspicious, as if the old lady would take her siesta. Should they creep out quietly? They sat in silence, uncertain, listening to the crackling of the fire and ticking off the mantelpiece clock.

Just as they were slowly rising from a sitting to a standing position, Lady Isabel's head sprang up, and she opened her eyes. They guiltily plonked down into their seats.

"I can't forget, my dear, the kindness you showed me in London. We had some lovely walks together, didn't we?"

"Yes, we did," Suzie agreed, flustered to find herself thus addressed.

"And I did you a great wrong," confessed Lady Isabel.

"Never mind," Suzie hastily reassured her.

Lady Isabel waved her lorgnettes and shook her head.

"But I do mind. My conscience has plagued me ever since. Within a few months, I realised you were correct in your assessment of Mr Biggs. But not before he had stolen vast amounts from the cellars. Last month, he was tried in a London court of justice, found guilty of theft, and transported to Australia."

Suzie gasped.

"But I am indebted to you, Miss Griffen. In my haste and under his obsequious spell, I dismissed you unjustly."

"That is all in the past, ma'am."

"So as may be, but I shall make amends," Lady Isabel replied, turning her attention to a pile of papers on her coffee table. Her sparkling rings clicked together, loose and large on her bony fingers.

She looked at Caleb: "Your father was put at immense personal risk when he took on the job of shepherd in Taitneach. I believe no one deemed it necessary to tell him any details of what he was letting himself into. That was very negligent." She turned to Suzie, "And your father has been a most dutiful and loyal tenant. I never forget speaking to him years ago at a tenants' annual dinner, and he told me he prayed for our family every day. Isn't that nice? The proposed union between the two of you brings together two of the best families on the estate."

"You tenants, of course, believe you know all about us and the estate, but…" She smiled mischievously, "some things we manage to keep under wraps." She picked up a wadge of paper.

"Many years ago, my late husband gifted me (mainly to perplex the tax man, you understand) several of the Brookfield farms, including Long Meadow and Dewbank. I am, as a matter of fact, your landlady."

Caleb and Suzie gasped.

"I have been deliberating how I could repay Miss Griffen. Then, when your letter of resignation came to my attention last week, I had great pleasure in concocting a little plan that would benefit both your families."

She patted the papers on her lap.

"I have decided to gift you with the two farms," she stated resolutely.

"But…" began Caleb.

"No ifs nor buts," commanded Lady Isabel, waving a silencing hand in his direction. "And so, you don't think this is just a doddery old lady's passing whim. I have had all the documents drawn up by my solicitor already. Here they are."

Maybe I've fallen asleep after all, and this is some outlandish dream. Suzie pinched herself—it hurt.

"Moreover, my longsuffering solicitor is waiting in the dining room to witness your signature, Mr Baker." She turned to Suzie, "Your father will need to come here tomorrow to sign his papers. I will send him a carriage."

Brushing aside their gasps and garbled thanks, she vigorously rang the bell for the solicitor to be summoned.

A businesslike air descended upon the room as Mr Edwards, the solicitor, rolled out maps of the farms and pointed out drainage systems and boundaries. He then moved on to the property deeds. Once Caleb had read and signed a few documents, Mr Edwards shook his hand. "Congratulations, young man; you are now the legal owner of Dewbank Farm."

Lady Isabel looked radiant but tired. After ringing the bell again, she requested a lie-down upstairs. Caleb and Suzie thanked her once again, and again, their gratitude was waved aside.

"The best thanks you can give me is to use this opportunity well and make a success of it," she instructed them as they left the room.

"We will do our very best," promised Caleb.

The housekeeper was all for ordering the coachman, but Caleb declined the offer.

"I think we would like to walk back, wouldn't we, Suzie?"

"Yes!" she agreed emphatically, then added, under her breath, "Or dance, hop, skip, and jump back!"

They walked sedately until they were around the corner, then sprang into each other's arms and yelled with delight..

"Can we…" Suzie began.

"Yes, we can!" beamed Caleb, "We can get married!"

"Does it really change everything?"

"Yes, it really does!" assured Caleb. "Without the monthly rent to pay, there is easily enough money coming in, even for the huge expense of a wife!"

They hugged for joy.

"And your father, free from that monthly outgoing, will feel liberated. He could use the money to hire help."

"So, you won't go to the Highlands?"

"No. Not as a bachelor. We can honeymoon there instead."

"How can we afford that?"

"My parents gave me the train fare when they first heard of our wedding plans. I thought I would be using it to return home, but now, it can be for its original use."

"How exciting!" Suzie squeezed his arm. "I am feeling quite dazed by all of this!"

By going down the woodman's track, they shortened their journey and avoided the village. Just as they were entering the coppicing wood, Caleb stopped.

"Before we reach home and tell your family, let's give the Lord thanks for everything."

So, embracing in a carpet of bluebells in the dappled sunlight, Caleb and Suzie added their voice of praise to the cheerful songs of the great tits and robins.

Printed in Great Britain
by Amazon